D0906305

GOVERNING
WITHOUT A MAJORITY

GOVERNING
WITHOUT
A MAJORITY

*Dilemmas for
Hung Parliaments in Britain*

DAVID BUTLER
Fellow of Nuffield College, Oxford

COLLINS
8 Grafton Street, London W1
1983

William Collins Sons and Co Ltd
London · Glasgow · Sydney · Auckland
Toronto · Johannesburg

British Library Cataloguing in Publication Data

Butler, David 1924
Governing without a majority.
1. Great Britain—Politics and government—1964-
I. Title
354. JN318

ISBN 0–00–217071–X

First published in 1983

© David Butler 1983

Photoset in Baskerville

Made and Printed in Great Britain
by William Collins Sons & Co Ltd, Glasgow

CONTENTS

LIST OF TABLES

PREFACE

Responsibility for the arguments contained in this book rests solely with the author. But a great many people have contributed to its contents. Vernon Bogdanor and I arranged a couple of one-day gatherings in Nuffield College (financed by the Parliamentary Democracy Trust) in order to explore the general problems that hung parliaments might present. I have drawn heavily on the papers which he and I prepared for those meetings and also on the ideas floated by those who attended one or both of them.

Alan Beith MP	David Marquand
Lord Blake	Austin Mitchell MP
John Curtice	Charles Morrison MP
Sammy Finer	Sir Michael Palliser
Sir Henry Fisher	Peter Pulzer
Sir John Herbecq	Geoffery Smith
Richard Holme	Michael Steed
Robert Jackson MEP	Anthony Teasdale
Paul McKee	William Wallace
David McKie	Philip Williams

My debt to Vernon Bogdanor is extreme. He helped me on many points, while working on his own independent contribution to the subject which will shortly be published. I also owe a special debt to John Curtice, not only for much of the material in Chapter 2, but also for his perceptive comments elsewhere. David Bradley, Dennis Kavanagh, Geoffrey Marshall, H. Berrington, James Mitchell, Hugh

Morison, and Chris Patten all read and improved my text. So too did Lord Blake, Sir John Herbecq, Peter Pulzer, Anthony Teasdale and Philip Williams among the conferees listed above. I should also acknowledge the very great help of Paul Jowett and of many colleagues in Nuffield College and elsewhere. Audrey Skeats persuaded a word processor to produce a manuscript that was in typography, if nothing else, immaculate.

NUFFIELD COLLEGE, OXFORD   NOVEMBER 1982

CHAPTER ONE

A Changing Constitution

THE PEOPLE OF BRITAIN have been accustomed to making a simple political choice. In each general election the voters have, effectively, been asked to decide which of two parties should govern. Over the last 50 years, with one slight exception, they have always sent a clear Conservative majority or a clear Labour majority to the House of Commons. Since 1945 every government has been formed entirely from one party. The King or Queen has never been faced with a real dilemma over who should be asked to be Prime Minister. Events have fostered in politicians, in civil servants, and in ordinary citizens a habit of mind that assumes the conduct of government to rest in the hands of a single party that commands a parliamentary majority.

But there is, of course, nothing inevitable about such a situation. Most of the democracies in the world have multi-party governments; indeed, many have had no experience of one party obtaining an absolute majority. And Britain in the 1980s is the scene of developments which make the uninterrupted continuance of the decisive majorities of the 1950s and 1960s more and more unlikely.

However, neither public opinion nor constitutional arrangements seem prepared for the problems that must arise when elections fail to produce clear decisions. If three parties emerge with roughly equal numbers of MPs, (and if, perhaps, several other significant groups are represented in Parliament), what will, or what should follow? What should the sovereign do? How should the party leaders react? And,

9

if a multi-party cabinet is formed, how will the practices of government differ from those to which everyone has been accustomed? Could the Prime Minister's powers be shared with a Deputy Prime Minister from another party? How would offices be distributed and departments run? And would the Prime Minister retain unfettered power to demand a dissolution of Parliament? A review of the possible situations opens up a host of questions, few of which can be answered in a simple or definitive way. Almost all the established rules of the political game would come under challenge, once single-party majority government ceased to be the norm. This book is an attempt to explore what the implications of such a situation might be.

It discusses how, when there is no clear majority in Parliament, a Prime Minister might be chosen and confirmed in office; how a government might be formed and the nature of any agreement between its supporters; how a coalition or a minority government might be conducted within the cabinet, within the departments, and within the House of Commons; and how it might end, either with or without a dissolution of Parliament.

It attempts to describe the existing guidelines on how the Palace and the potential Prime Ministers, as well as the other politicians and the party organizations, should go about handling a situation of which Britain has only limited experience.

But, before plunging into a discussion of hypothetical problems that have not yet arisen, it is worth looking at the situation we have already reached. All works on British government are necessarily out of date. With an unwritten constitution we rely on precedent. When analysing a problem or a procedure the experts describe what was done the last time it arose. But often there is no recent example to draw upon. The textbooks are littered with precedents that are no longer be relevant. Few people realize the extent to which the rules of the game that held good, even twenty years ago, have become hopelessly out of date and inappropriate.

Consider the following sentence which in 1960, or even perhaps in 1970, most people would have accepted as an accurate, if portentous, statement of the bases of British government:

> Britain is (1) *governed* under (2) *an unwritten constitution* based on a (3) *fused* and (4) *centralized* system by a (5) *Cabinet* (6) *collectively responsible* and (7) *individually responsible* to a (8) *sovereign parliament*, dominated by (9) *two parties* chosen (10) *first past the post*, by a (11) *stable electorate*.

Every one of the numbered points in that sentence has come under challenge in the last generation.

1 Britain is governed.   People have become sceptical about how far any government really governs. Four alternations in party control over twenty years have had remarkably small effect on the broad trends of national life. Our fate is far more influenced by our existing industrial structure and habits, by the continuing attitudes of civil servants, and by international circumstances than it is by any policy switches that a simple change of ministers can, in practice, bring about. We have lost some of our respect for authority and we have become more realistic about the limits of the possible for any government.

2 An unwritten constitution.   Through membership of the European Community, and through subscription to the quite separate European Convention of Human Rights, Britain has acquired some elements of a written constitution. Moreover influential figures, such as Lord Hailsham and Lord Scarman, have committed themselves in favour of a written constitution and a Bill of Rights. Lord Wade's Bill of Rights has twice been passed by the House of Lords. Britain is still a long way from the other democracies of the world, almost all of which have a written constitution incorporating some elements of a Bill of Rights. But written constitutions and Bills of Rights have, in the last decade, become a significant part of British political discussion.

3 Fused government. In our unwritten constitution there is no separation of powers between executive, legislature and judiciary of the kind so evident in the United States. All authority is fused in a cabinet answerable to Parliament which can amend any law that the courts interpret awkwardly. But the fused nature of British government is under challenge. Some executive and some legislative powers have been transferred to the European Community; the British government and British citizens are subject to the Community courts, as well as to the quite separate European Court of Human Rights. Domestically, too, the courts have become much more active and, for various reasons, the number of cases with real political significance has vastly increased, not only in the highly-charged industrial relations field but also in routine matters such as Laker Airways, Tameside Schools and London Transport fares.

Moreover, the various proposals for reforming the British state – a written constitution and a Bill of Rights, as well as devolution to the regions – would each open up the possibility of formalized conflict between separated institutions of government; some form of judicial review would inevitably be involved in the settlement of such conflicts.

Even the separation of powers between executive and legislature through a cabinet answerable to, but in control of, the House of Commons is under challenge. When governments lack assured majorities, Parliament comes into its own: the cabinet has to accept adverse votes and it has to listen to Select Committees. So far, any battles between Downing Street and Westminster have been very muted compared to the continuous struggle between the White House and Capitol Hill. But the situation is changing.

4 Centralized government. The very centralized,

London-based, nature of British government has come under challenge, in one direction through our accession to the European Community, with jurisdiction over many matters moving to Brussels, and in another direction, through the demands for devolution to Scotland, Wales, and even to parts of England. If a few thousand Scotsmen had voted differently in the 1979 referendum, we would now have a Scottish regional assembly. Even without that, much administration has moved to Edinburgh, and in recent years to Cardiff. Moreover, all parties pay lip-service to further devolution and greater autonomy for local government. Britain still has a London-dominated government, but, if policy declarations mean anything, that is likely to become less and less the case.

5 Cabinet government.   Britain still has cabinet government. But the idea that all the important decisions of government emerge from the collective deliberations of twenty or so politicians arguing together around the table at 10 Downing Street has been in large measure dissipated. Often the cabinet can only rubber-stamp the recommendations of small sub-committees, and often the Prime Minister can by-pass the cabinet altogether. We can now see that the traditional picture of how the cabinet works is far from the current practice, even if we do not agree with R.H.S. Crossman's assertion that cabinet government has been replaced by Prime Ministerial government.

6 Collective responsibility.   Collective cabinet responsibility remains one of the most important principles underpinning British government. But its meaning has certainly changed. The 1975 referendum on Europe provides the extreme example of the extent to which the notion that all key decisions are made by an ostensibly united cabinet can be attenuated: this major issue was referred from cabinet (and Parliament) to the electorate and the cabinet was openly divided on it. Moreover, in 1974-9 the government accepted defeat on a number of issues that once would have been treated as issues of confidence and resignation. But, more generally, the falling-off in official secrecy and the increasing number of cabinet leaks illustrate a continued erosion of collective responsibility as a constraint on participants in the governing process.

7 Individual responsibility. Individual ministerial responsibility, the doctrine by which a minister has to answer to Parliament for every act of a civil servant, has also come under threat. The increasing size of government makes a farce of the idea that ministers can personally control or manage their departments in any thoroughgoing way. Ministers have become more ready to make scapegoats of civil servants when things go wrong. Civil servants have become more public figures, making speeches, appearing before Select Committees and even venturing on television. Their utterances, in a characteristically 'mandarin' way, often reveal how much it is they who run the country.

8 A sovereign Parliament. The absolute sovereignty of Parliament has been directly curtailed by British membership of the Common Market. Directives made by the Commission and the Council of Ministers in Brussels can pass automatically into Community law without any ratification by the parliaments of the member states. The sovereignty of Parliament would be still further curtailed if the freedom of MPs to pass any law they chose were circumscribed, as it would have to be, by any serious move towards devolution or towards a written constitution or indeed towards the use of referendums. Moreover, independent of any formal modification of its sovereignty, the effective authority of Parliament over the processes of government is widely seen as in decline.

9 A two-party system. From 1950 to 1970 the country remained firmly in the grip of a two-party system: 98 per cent of MPs elected were from the Conservative or Labour parties and 93 per cent of all votes cast went to those parties. But in the three elections of 1974-9 the situation changed. The two big parties secured only 94 per cent of MPs and only 77 per cent of the votes. This was because Northern Ireland moved outside the mainland party system while nationalists were elected in Scotland and Wales, and, most important, the Liberal vote leapt up. Since then, the Alliance of Liberals and Social Democrats has been formed. Its unprecedented by-election successes in the winter of 1981-2 suggested that even bigger third-party breakthroughs were at least possible. This book is about the implications of any collapse of two-party dominance for the operation of British government.

10 First-past-the-post elections.   First-past-the-post elections have been an essential element in the two-party dominance. The traditional British system encourages voters to concentrate their support on that party of the leading two which they dislike least. Those who have sought to change the system have been a small, if at times vocal, minority. But in the last decade there has been a growing tendency to talk of other systems. The European Community and the possibility of a common electoral system for the European Parliament has focused attention on proportional representation (PR). The problems of Northern Ireland have led British governments of both complexions to sponsor PR within the United Kingdom. And there has been an increase in public awareness that Britain is one of a very few democracies that continues to adhere to first-past-the-post elections. It seems far less certain than it did a decade ago that first-past-the-post elections will still be a part of the British scene by the year 2000.

11 A stable electorate.   The essential reason why first-past-the-post elections did not produce violent oscillations in the 1950s and 1960s was the stability of the British voter.

Governments did change hands in 1951, 1964 and 1970 but on modest swings. Over twenty years, the average net movement between the main parties from one election to the next was only 2.5 per cent. In the 1950s it was a mere 1.5 per cent. But the stable electorate of that period, with the bulk of voters set in their traditional loyalty to Conservative or to Labour, has now disintegrated. Since the mid-1960s by-elections, local elections and opinion polls have shown ever greater oscillations in party support. In the first half of 1982 all records for volatility were broken when the proportion intending to vote Conservative rose from 27 per cent to 48 per cent, while Alliance support (which had risen so spectacularly in the previous year) fell from 44 per cent to 22 per cent. When movements on this scale can take place in so short a space of time, it is nonsense to speak of 'the stable British electorate'.

This catalogue of change in, or questioning of, long-established practice shows how new thinking is needed in all areas – and not just in those upon which the attention of this book is focused. Of course, the system has its own momentum. Many of these challenges, at least for the time being, have come to little or nothing. Yet they have been strong enough to induce a new sense of uncertainty, a new questioning of the conventions under which we are governed. And in many circumstances it is no longer clear what these conventions are; there is no agreement on the proper course of action when a crisis arises. Moreover there is no authority possessed of the unquestioned status to lay down answers. The forming of coalition or minority governments presents one special area where Britain is likely to stumble into situations in which, perforce, those who have to act will act arbitrarily; and in which, consequently, those who lose out are likely to cry 'foul' and to throw doubt on the legitimacy of the outcome.

There is no change that would have more far-reaching implications for our political system than for hung parliaments to become the norm. We fail to realize the extent to which all our assumptions about the working of Parliament and government, and indeed about the nature of politics itself, are based upon the assumption that two dominant parties will alternate between government and opposition in Britain. We have become inured to politics as a team game, a battle between traditional rivals. The image is reinforced by the rectangular chamber of the House of Commons with cabinet and shadow cabinet facing each other in near proximity and their back-benchers just behind them, cheering them on. There are the two division lobbies, with every vote on a substantial matter seen as a vote of confidence on which the life of the government and indeed of the parliament depends. The efforts of the whips and the traditions of collective cabinet responsibility reinforce conventional images of politics as an adversarial rather than a co-operative activity. In Britain, as everywhere else, politics is the art of compromise, of finding the least bad solution, or at least the one that upsets fewest people. But the compromise between the main protagonists tends not to be visible: all issues are seen as a question of government victory or defeat. Once governments cease to be based on single-party majorities, the process of compromise has to become visible. Coalition partners have to agree not to press for everything in their own party manifesto. Minority governments have, on each successive issue, to square some MPs from the other parties. For good or ill, open negotiation and argument would become the order of the day.

There has been much talk recently about 'breaking the mould' of British politics. But in one sense it has already been broken and in another it is indestructible. It has been broken by the increased volatility of the British voter who in this generation has become far less prone to adhere faithfully to a single political party. It has also been broken by changes in the values and authority structure of the parties; the confrontation between Conservative and Labour has become sharper: all parties, but the Labour party especially, have undergone great and disruptive changes. The consequences are far-reaching. After 1979 British politics could not have returned to a bipartisan Butskellism, even if the SDP and the Alliance had never come into being. And now, even if the Alliance loses its appeal, other challenges to the old two party alternation are likely to arise.

On the other hand, even if the Alliance's challenge succeeds completely and brings about all the institutional changes it has foreshadowed, British politics will continue much the same. The national dilemmas will not be altered and their solution will remain largely beyond the remedy of even the most enlightened government. The new politicians will resemble the old. They will be fallible human beings, cross-pressured by self-interest and idealism, by party demands and administrative realities.

In the autumn of 1981 the newly formed Liberal/SDP Alliance was at the top of the polls and winning almost every by-election. The scale of the third party upsurge was unprecedented. The Alliance, more than anything else in the past 50 years, raised the possibility that multi-party politics had come to stay. It was a challenge which provided the genesis of this book. Yet the relevance of these pages does not depend on the immediate, and perhaps ephemeral, situation. It is being written in the autumn of 1982 when no one can say whether the Alliance is already a spent force or whether circumstances will give it a new upsurge; but the arguments here are not tied to what happens in any particular election or to the success, or even to the survival, of the current third-party grouping. The likelihood that, at some point within a decade, Britain will have a hung parliament is, as the next chapter will argue, very considerable; the likelihood is also considerable that at least by the end of the century we shall join the rest of Europe in adopting proportional representation – a change in our institutions which will make hung parliaments the norm rather than the exception. That Britain will, within the foreseeable future, face the problems dealt with in these pages is not a remote contingency; it is a high probability.

Perhaps at the outset of such a work, it is important to stress what the book is not. It is not:

A forecast that the next election will produce a hung parliament.

An advocacy of, or an attack on, proportional representation.

A defence of, or an attack on, adversary politics.

An advocacy of specific changes in constitutional practice.

However, the aims of the pages that follow can be set out positively. The book is:

An exploration of how likely it is that a multi-party situation will arise.

An examination of the problems that a multi-party situation would produce, particularly if it seemed likely that further elections would not end the multi-party situation.

An advocacy of further consideration of these problems, undertaken by everyone concerned well in advance of any such development.

What will be apparent from these pages is that the past offers no adequate guide to certain specific dilemmas which the nation may face before long. It will also become plain that there are no obvious or easy answers.

CHAPTER TWO

Electoral Systems
and Hung Parliaments

———•○•———

ONE TITLE SUGGESTED for this book was *Life After PR*. It is, after
all, an exploration of the problems that would necessarily
follow if proportional representation were adopted. Proportional representation would virtually guarantee that there
would never again be a clear majority for one party. But *Life
After PR* as a simple and arresting title for the book would
have been misleading because, despite popular belief, even
the existing electoral system does not guarantee clear
majorities. Proportional representation is a sufficient but not
a necessary condition for hung parliaments. Indeed, as this
chapter will argue, first-past-the-post elections are increasingly likely to produce them. The book's central focus is on
governing without majorities and not on the mechanics of
the electoral system. Yet a consideration of how the existing
electoral system currently operates to translate votes into
seats, and of how a proportional system might work is
essential to the argument.

The British electoral system has traditionally been
credited with the supreme virtue of providing decisive
results; it discourages minor parties, forcing voters to choose
between alternative governments, and it gives a clear
majority to the winner. There has not been an election since
the war in which a party has won 50 per cent of the total vote
– yet in every election save one a single party has secured
over half the seats in the House of Commons. The movement
in votes from one election to the next has been small. Over
the last ten contests the swings between the two main parties

20

have averaged 2.5 per cent (with a range between 1 per cent and 5 per cent); but the shifts in seats have been much larger, averaging 8 per cent (with a range between 3 per cent and 12 per cent). This exaggerated link between seats and votes has been encapsulated in the simple proposition of the Cube Law: if votes are divided between two parties in the ratio A:B, seats will be divided in the ratio $A^3:B^3$. On this basis, in a 600 seat parliament with two evenly balanced parties, a 1 per cent swing in votes will change the outcome in 18 seats making a difference of 36 to the majority; a 3 per cent swing could make the difference between a tied parliament and a majority of over 100 seats. This indeed was what happened in 1966. At the minimum level, in 1951 a 0.9 per cent swing from Labour to Conservative sufficed to transform a Labour government with a clear overall majority of six into a Conservative government with a clear overall majority of seventeen.

In the 1950s and 1960s the Cube Law continued to operate as a convenient, if oversimplified, explanation of the relation between seats and votes, as a reason why parties which never secured a majority in votes regularly secured a majority in seats.

But, although few people realize it, the Cube Law no longer works and hung parliaments have become far more likely. This is not just because of the upsurge of third parties over the last decade (though we shall return to that). Even if third party support had stayed at the negligible level of the 1950s, the Cube Law would have become less and less valid.

The number of marginal seats has declined and the number of safe seats has increased. In 1955, 172 seats were held by Labour or Conservative with majorities of under 10 per cent; in 1979 the comparable figure was only 127. Fewer seats are now at risk from any given swing.

The main explanation seems to lie in demographic developments that have little to do with the party political struggle. Rural areas have become far more Conservative. Urban centres have become far more Labour. Scotland and the north of England have moved clearly to the left while the south of England and the Midlands have moved clearly to the right.

Table 1 shows how the Conservative share of votes has changed.[1]

TABLE 1
Change in Conservative share of two-party votes 1955-1979

GB	South and Midlands	North of England	Scotland	City seats	Very Rural seats
+1·5	+6·4	−2·9	−8·7	−5·9	+10·1

There is a net difference of 15 per cent between the south and Scotland in the movement of party support; there is a similar difference between the most urban and the most rural areas. And that, as Table 2 shows, makes a big difference, geographically, to the balance of representation.

TABLE 2
Conservative share of seats in various regions 1955 and 1979

		GB	South and Midlands	North of England	Scotland
Seats (%)	1955	54%	63%	48%	51%
	1979	54%	72%	35%	31%
Turnover	1955-79	—	+9%	−13%	−20%

The Conservatives have gained heavily in their strong areas (rural seats and the south) and have lost ground in their weak areas (the city centres, the north of England and Scotland).

East Anglian seats – like South-West Norfolk and Lowestoft – which were once Labour marginals have become safely Conservative. But the Conservatives have had difficulty in holding a single seat in Liverpool or Manchester which, in the 1950s, had roughly equal Conservative and Labour representation. Glasgow which had seven Conservative members in 1955 had none by 1982; by 1982, also, after three defections to the Social Democrats, Labour had no MPs south of a line drawn from Battersea to Bristol.

One by-product of this long-term trend has been to make the Conservative and Labour parliamentary parties more sectional, less representative of the whole nation. The voice of the urban north comes to Conservative governments through internal party channels less strongly than it used to; the countryside now sends hardly any Labour MPs to lobby a Labour government. Such developments raise issues beyond our present argument. But one consequence worth noting is that, when the rival parliamentary parties come to represent more completely differentiated segments of the community, they may find it harder to work together in a coalition than in a situation where a larger proportion of them have to appeal to broadly similar marginal seats in every part of the country.

The fact that fewer seats change hands for any given movement of votes increases the likelihood of a hung parliament. We have moved from a Cube Law to a Square Law (if votes are divided A:B, seats will be divided $A^2:B^2$) so that now with two evenly balanced parties, ten seats rather than eighteen will switch for each 1 per cent swing. The chances of any general election yielding a result that falls in the middle ground, in that no man's land of no majority, have been greatly enhanced.

Moreover, the no man's land has already been much enlarged for quite other reasons. Between 1950 and 1970 most parliaments contained fewer than ten minor party MPs (as Table 3 shows). Now there are bound to be more; the reason lies in three separate developments.

Events in Northern Ireland have meant that the province (which once had all its twelve members under the Conservative umbrella) will not, in the foreseeable future, send to Westminster MPs who can be categorized as part of a mainland party. The twelve Northern Irish seats have been increased to seventeen. These seventeen MPs from the six counties (however much they are divided one against another) will constitute an independent element in any future Parliament.

Scottish and Welsh nationalism have also advanced. The Scottish National Party and Plaid Cymru may be unlikely to drive out the London-centred parties from their countries but they have established a bridgehead from which they are unlikely to be totally dislodged. One or two Plaid Cymru members will probably be returned from the five or six predominantly Welsh speaking constituencies. The Scottish Nationalists, with one secure seat in the Western Isles, also stand poised within range of a breakthrough in various parts of mainland Scotland. It seems reasonable to assume that a future Parliament (like the present one) will contain at least three or four Welsh and Scottish Nationalists – and the possibility of a much bigger contingent cannot be ruled out.

The third extension of the no man's land is, potentially, the largest. The Liberals barely survived the 1950s but each of their recurrent revivals since 1959 has added to their bridgehead. Their local organization has grown and been consolidated by local government successes so that, if they still lack many secure seats, they are in a situation where their total elimination is unlikely; their potential for a massive breakthrough, in company with their new SDP allies, remains appreciable. There is no point in speculating here on Alliance prospects which, in a single year, have seen such spectacular rises and declines. What is plain is that, in this volatile world, they must continue to be taken seriously.

There is one other possible source of MPs outside the main parties. In the 1970s, for the first time since the war, party rebels achieved electoral success. S.O.Davies in 1970, Dick Taverne in 1972 and 1974, and Eddie Milne in 1974 stood against the Labour party in their old constituencies and won. It is at least possible that this pattern may be repeated – and on a larger scale.

Taking all these factors together, it seems hard to envisage a Parliament that does not contain, at the very minimum, 25 MPs with no attachment to the Conservative or Labour parties. A more plausible rock-bottom figure might be 35, with 17 from Northern Ireland, 4 Welsh and Scottish Nationalists and 14 supplied by Liberals, Social Democrats and party rebels.

In 6 of the last 10 elections, 35 other members would have been enough to hold the balance of power, as Table 3 shows. Even without taking account of the upsurge of the Alliance or of the changes that have affected the working of the electoral system, the likelihood of no party having a clear majority has become much greater than a generation ago. When a Parliament contains 30 minor party members, it is 3 times as likely to be 'hung' as when there are 10.

Curtice and Steed have calculated that, making allowance for the current performance of the electoral system but, assuming no third-party advance beyond 1979 levels, any election in which Conservative and Labour shares of the two-party vote[2] fall within 3.5 per cent of each other is liable to produce a hung parliament. On their calculations at least four of the last ten elections would nowadays have led to a hung parliament and a further two would have yielded an overall majority of less than twenty.

TABLE 3
Results and majorities 1950-79

	Con	Lab	Lib	Other	Total minor parties	Gap between Con and Lab	Clear majority
1950	298	315	9	3	12	17	5
1951	321	295	6	3	9	26	17
1955	344	277	6	3	9	67	58
1959	365	258	6	1	7	107	100
1964	304	317	9	–	9	13	4
1966	253	363	12	2	14	110	96
1970	330	287	6	7	13	43	30
1974 F	297	301	14	23	37	4	33
1974 O	277	319	13	26	39	42	3
1979	339	269	11	16	27	70	43

These calculations are on the basis of the two-party vote. But consider in a more simplistic way, the actual percentage margins between the two big parties in the total UK vote.

TABLE 4
Gap in votes between Conservative and Labour 1950-79

	Conservative % lead over Labour	Swing needed to produce equal votes
1950	−2·6	1·3
1951	+0·8	0·4
1955	+3·3	1·7
1959	+5·6	2·8
1964	−0·7	0·4
1966	−6·0	3·0
1970	+3·4	1·7
1974 F	+0·8	0·4
1974 O	−3·4	1·7
1979	+7·0	3·5

Table 4 shows how narrowly balanced post-war elections have been and how small a movement would have been needed to change the victor in any of them.

In seven out of ten elections a 2 per cent swing would have put the other party into the lead. If the United Kingdom is now in a situation where only 10 seats change hands for every 1 per cent swing and where there are at least 30 seats in minor party hands, it is easy to see that the probability of a hung parliament has become very high. The matter can be put schematically. Table 5 makes the plausible assumption that third parties with 20 per cent of the vote win 30 seats and that, after redistribution, the electoral system has no bias as between Conservative and Labour in a 650 seat Parliament. It shows graphically that, on this basis there will be no clear majority unless the parties are separated by at least 3 per cent. Unless one has a lead of at least 4 per cent (which since the war has happened only in 1959, 1966, and 1979) the majority would be under ten – quite insufficient to guarantee a five-year parliament under the control of a single party.

The point can be made simply in three propositions.

1 If lesser parties get a total of 30 seats (e.g. Northern Irish 17, Welsh and Scottish Nationalists 3, Alliance 10), one of the big parties must secure a 4 per cent lead in votes over the other to secure a working majority of 10 seats. Only three out of the last ten elections have produced such a lead.

2 If lesser parties get a total of 50 seats (e.g. Northern Irish 17, Welsh and Scottish Nationalists 5, Alliance 30), one of the big parties must secure a 6 per cent lead over the other to get a clear majority of seats. Only one out of the last ten elections has produced such a lead.

3 If lesser parties get a total of 70 seats, one of the big parties must secure an 8 per cent lead in votes over the other to get a working majority. No party since 1945 has enjoyed an 8 per cent lead in votes.

TABLE 5

Five hypothetical pictures of votes and seats

			100	200	300	325
	Votes	*Seats*				
Con	42%	330				
Others	20%	30				
Lab	38%	290				
Con	41%	320				
Others	20%	30				
Lab	39%	300				
Con	40%	310				
Others	20%	30				
Lab	40%	310				
Con	39%	300				
Others	20%	30				
Lab	41%	320				
Con	38%	290				
Others	20%	30				
Lab	42%	330				

These three propositions assume that the two big parties are faring equally at the hands of the electoral system. It is possible that, if the third party made a big advance, the

TABLE 6
Five scenarios for three-way outcomes

A   Conservative working majority

	Con	Lab	Lib/SDP	NI
Major party votes (GB)	39%	33%	28%	–
Seats	334	264	35	17

B   Labour working majority

	Con	Lab	Lib/SDP	NI
Major party vote (GB)	31%	36%	33%	–
Seats	215	334	84	17

C   Alliance working majority

	Con	Lab	Lib/SDP	NI
Major party vote (GB)	33%	25%	42%	–
Seats	127	172	334	17

D   Conservative-Labour deadlock

	Con	Lab	Lib/SDP	NI
Major party vote (GB)	36%	35%	29%	–
Seats	292	298	43	17

E   Three-way split

	Con	Lab	Lib/SDP	NI
Major party vote (GB)	34%	27%	39%	–
Seats	235	223	175	17

The figures in Table 6 are based on the assumption of uniform swings from the 1979 results. The likely effects of redistribution, which will produce a 650 seat Parliament and is worth about 20 seats' gain to the Conservatives, are allowed for. For simplicity the Nationalists and any Independents are excluded.

system would, at the critical point, be skewed in favour of Labour (as is shown in Table 6). But, even if allowance were made for this in a more complex reformulation of the propositions set out above, it would not upset the central argument: it is plain that there is a very wide band where even a substantial lead by one of the big parties over the other would not be sufficient to yield a clear majority.

Moreover, there is reason to believe that the demographic trends which have changed the working of the electoral system are still continuing. If this is so, by the late 1980s there will be fewer marginals. The range of outcomes that will yield a hung parliament will be even wider.

All of this argument can be summed up in a simple assertion: even if there is no large-scale third-party break-through there is, under the existing system, at least an even chance that a general election will produce a hung parliament.

Let us now add two further possibilities – a major third party advance and the adoption of proportional representation.

The first-past-the-post electoral system can be very hard on minority parties and it can give greatly exaggerated majorities to the winner. But at least it has been reasonably fair as between the two big parties. The party that has won most votes has won most seats (give or take 1 per cent). In the 1950s the system was, by geographic accident, slightly skewed in favour of the Conservatives (and they won the 1951 election although Labour got 0.6 per cent more votes); in the 1970s it was slightly skewed in favour of Labour (they got four more seats in the February 1974 election although they had 0.8 per cent fewer votes). But these limited irregularities, to which PR systems are also subject, have not been a major source of grievance.

If, however, there were a serious third party challenge, the irregularities could become much worse. It is interesting to calculate what would have happened in 1979 in a three-way tie. If in every constituency 12.3 per cent of Conservative support and 5.3 per cent of Labour support had been transferred to the Liberals, each of the three parties would have had the same share of the national vote, 31.6 per cent. But the Labour party would have got 302 seats, the Conservatives 242 and the Liberals 66. The Liberal disadvantage is largely accounted for by the fact that Liberal strength is spread so evenly: they would win lots of second places but few first places. The milder Conservative handicap can be explained on the grounds that such seats as the Liberals won would almost all be at Conservative expense.

Table 6 set out five scenarios which underline the point. In these hypothetical adaptations from the 1979 result, it is shown that Labour could get a working majority with 36 per cent of the vote; the Conservatives need 39 per cent; and the Alliance needs 42 per cent. In the last scenario the Alliance with 12 per cent more of the vote than Labour would have almost 50 fewer seats.

Inequitable results of this sort could have a major impact on the moral authority of a government and they could certainly influence positions in any inter-party bargaining. They would also add to the pressure for electoral reform. When an electoral system works with conspicuous unfairness, not just to minor parties but also to some of the leading actors on the political scene, public agitation for change is likely to grow sharply. Not only would the demonstrated case for proportional representation be much strengthened but there would be major forces with a vested interest in a new system.

Proportional representation, if adopted, would have a far reaching impact on the working of British politics. Hung parliaments, already an increasing possibility under first-past-the-post voting, would become an established certainty.

There are many forms of proportional representation and

their consequences are diverse and beyond the scope of this book. But, since we are considering how hung parliaments should be handled, with or without PR, it is necessary to stress what PR would do:

1 It would give a virtual guarantee that no party would ever win a clear majority.

2 Consequently, it would reduce the likelihood that a dissolution would solve a political deadlock.

3 It would damp down changes in representation, giving MPs, provided they could secure renomination, more assured careers and less fear of elections.

4 It would give minor parties a better chance of representation and increase the possibility of break-aways from the major parties.

These propositions would hold under almost any variant of proportional representation. But the actual form can make a great difference. Some, such as the List Systems of Scandinavia and the Low Countries, or the Additional Member System of West Germany, would add to the power of the party machines. On the other hand, the Single Transferable Vote on the Irish model would probably foster a constituency-focused individualism among MPs.

If proportional representation were to be adopted, it would certainly encourage people to switch votes from Conservative and Labour to third or minor parties. And since, in the last three elections, 44 per cent of the vote has been the most that either big party has obtained, it may be reasonable to presume that neither would again top that figure, let alone approach the 50 per cent needed for a parliamentary majority under a pure proportional system.

However, while most democracies have PR systems, few have sought perfect proportionality. Most systems have an implicit or an explicit threshold below which a minor party is denied representation. In Germany this is set formally at

5 per cent of the vote. In Ireland it ranges from 17 per cent to 25 per cent in its variously-sized constituencies. Some votes are therefore wasted in any system by being given to candidates who cannot be elected; thus the larger parties enjoy a slightly higher percentage of seats than their vote would entitle them to. In 1953 Germany had a single party majority based on 45 per cent of the vote. In 1969 Ireland had one based on 46 per cent. In 1979 Italy, with a very proportional system, gave the Christian Democrats 41.5 per cent of the seats with 38.4 per cent of the votes.

Moreover some proportional systems contain anomalies which produce bizarre outcomes. Consider the two Irish results in Table 7.

TABLE 7
Irish elections 1969 and 1973

	1969 Votes	Seats	1973 Votes	Seats
Fianna Fail	45·7%	75	46·2%	69
Fine Gael	34·2% } 51·1%	50 } 68	35·1% } 48·8%	54 } 73
Lab	16·9%	18	13·7%	19
Others	3·2%	1	5·0%	2

Fianna Fail won the election and formed the government in 1969; it improved its vote in 1973, and yet it lost office to the Fine Gael/Labour coalition whose vote had dropped[3]. And less extreme anomalies can be cited from the different proportional systems used in Norway and Sweden.

However imperfect, any form of PR would produce more proportional results than a first-past-the-post system. Yet it would not necessarily add to the number of parties. German voters in the six elections from 1961 to 1980 returned only three parties to the Bundestag. Ireland, in addition to its three main parties, has sometimes had only one outsider MP, despite a system peculiarly open to individualist candidates. There is little likelihood of Britain adopting a system like that in the Netherlands or in Italy which positively encourages the multiplication of parties.

PR would probably affect the relative strength of the parties at Westminster far more than their number. But the nature of the minority or coalition governments that followed would be influenced by the extent to which the system adopted was one which fostered or discouraged central party authority as against localist individualism, and by the extent to which it affected the possibilities of party splits.

PR would transform elections and politics in Britain and make hung parliaments a certainty. But, even without PR, the working of the electoral system and of British politics is changing fast. Hung parliaments are becoming a probability rather than a possibility. How should we cope with them? Let us first look at how we have coped with them in the past, and then at how, in their various ways, other countries have managed the situation.

CHAPTER THREE

Past British Experience

———◦○◦———

BECAUSE BRITAIN has an unwritten constitution, the management of her affairs is at the mercy of precedent. The rules governing proper constitutional conduct are based on what was done, or thought to have been done, last time – if there was a last time. Unfortunately there is no constitutional court, no established authority to determine what was actually done last time or whether it remains relevant. Historians, constitutional lawyers and politicians each form their own ideas of what essential principles were at stake in the key examples from the past and then each lays down what should now be regarded as correct.

This kind of *ad hoc* approach is inevitable and not necessarily undesirable. Yet it is bound to lead to confusion. This book is an attempt to sort out some of the uncertainties inherent in one particular type of crisis. Its aim is not to give authoritative answers – that would be impossible – but to draw attention to some of the most relevant precedents, in a way that may help to clarify future arguments and even accelerate the solution of crises.

Twentieth-century British politics certainly offers plenty of precedents that bear on coalition and minority government. Some of them are still the subject of fierce historical controversy; some, as we approach the twenty-first century, have plainly become obsolete. Yet there are many points where, in future crises, good or bad examples drawn from the last 80 years will certainly be cited as binding. It is worth looking briefly at this century's experience of minority and coalition governments.

Five of the twenty-one general elections in this century have failed to produce a clear majority, and one yielded a margin so small that, for the second half of a five-year Parliament, the government was in a minority. On each occasion the outcome was a single-party minority government. But on four other occasions, none of them following a general election, a perceived need to seek national unity in a crisis led to the formation of a coalition.

As Table 8 shows, single-party majority government has prevailed for only 43 years of this century. However, if we add those governments that were coalitions in name only (because one party was firmly in the saddle and had a majority on its own), the proportion rises to 56 years out of 82. Furthermore, for ten of the thirteen years where the coalition was genuine, one party still had a clear majority. There remain twelve years of minority rule.

TABLE 8

Nature of British governments 1900-82

A *Single-party clear majority government* (53% of the period)

		Years	Months
Jan 1906-Jan 1910	Liberal	4	0
Oct 1922-Dec 1923	Conservative	1	2
Oct 1924-May 1929	Conservative	4	7
Jul 1945-Oct 1951	Labour	6	3
Oct 1951-Oct 1964	Conservative	13	0
Oct 1964-Jun 1970	Labour	5	8
Jun 1970-Feb 1974	Conservative	3	8
Oct 1974-Mar 1976	Labour	1	5
May 1979-(Dec 1982)	Conservative	3	7
		43	4

B *Coalition but one party in a clear majority (and other components moving toward fusion)* (16% of the period)

Jul 1900-Dec 1905	Conservative/Liberal Unionist	5	5
Sep 1932-May 1940	National Government (basically Conservative)	7	8
May 1945-Jul 1945	'Caretaker' Government (basically Conservative)	0	2
		13	3

C *Genuine coalition government* (17% of the period)

May 1915-Oct 1922	Wartime coalition continuing under Liberal PM (even after Conservative majority in Dec 1918)	7	5
Aug 1931-Sep 1932	National Government	1	1
May 1940-May 1945	Wartime coalition despite clear Conservative majority	5	0
		13	6

D *Single-party minority rule* (14% of the period)

Jan 1910-May 1915	Liberal dependent on Irish Nats (but usually having Labour support too)	5	4
Jan 1924-Oct 1924	Labour dependent on Liberals	–	9
May 1929-Aug 1931	Labour dependent on Liberals	2	3
Mar 1974-Oct 1974	Labour dependent on all other parties not uniting to defeat them	–	7
Mar 1976-May 1979	Labour dependent on all other parties not uniting to defeat them (except during Lab-Lib pact Mar 77-Aug 78)	3	2
		12	1

No election which failed to produce a clear majority has led to a coalition; in these situations one party has always gone it alone as a minority government, usually without any explicit understanding with another grouping. Only briefly, in 1931, has Britain had experience in time of peace of an authentic coalition, made up of genuinely independent parties.

None the less, the exceptions to single-party majority rule offer significant guidance on the problems with which this book is concerned. Many of these will be referred to in later chapters. But here we shall explore briefly the establishment and the downfall of each coalition and each minority government and draw attention to some of their special features.

1895-1905

By 1900 the Conservative/Liberal Unionist coalition was well launched on the road to the party fusion that was to be completed in 1912. The diverse group of Whigs and Radicals who had broken with Gladstone over Home Rule had joined the Conservatives in government in 1895; they were allotted a slightly more than proportionate share of cabinet ministers (17 per cent of coalition MPs, 26 per cent of the offices) even though their support was not absolutely necessary to give the Conservatives power. But Salisbury, the Conservative Prime Minister, was well aware that Joseph Chamberlain and the Duke of Devonshire were politicians of great influence. The parties continued to function separately throughout the 1895-1905 administration and preserved separate whips' offices. But when, in fact, the government was split over Tariff Reform in 1903, the Conservatives and Liberal Unionist parties were equally riven. Indeed the fact that the government was a coalition had nothing to do with its coming to an end in December 1905.

The cement of the Conservative/Liberal Unionist alliance

was, of course, an electoral understanding which went back to 1886. Once they had united electorally in order to oust Gladstone, it was very difficult to break apart, for had they fought each other in the constituencies they would have presented a large number of seats to the Liberals.

If the 1895-1905 coalition has a lesson for the present day it is surely that sustained partnership tends towards fusion when it has its roots in the necessities of first-past-the-post elections.

1906-15

The results of the elections on which Liberal rule from 1906-15 was based, set out in Table 9, tell a simple story.

TABLE 9

Election results 1906 and 1910

	Seats				Parliamentary majority		
	Con	Lib	Lab	Irish Nat	Lib over Con	Lib over all others	
Jan 1906	157	400	30	83	243	130	670 *seats*
Jan 1910	273	275	40	82	2	−120	336 *needed for*
Dec 1910	272	272	42	84	−	−126	*majority*

From 1906-10 the Liberals received Irish and Labour support generally, even though they did not need it. The Irish could never hope to extract Home Rule from the Conservative/Liberal Unionist coalition. The Labour party, though it had an independent base in the trade unions and a firm hold on some industrial seats, owed a large part of its parliamentary strength to the deal between MacDonald and the Liberals which gave Labour a clear run in most of the seats they won.

After 1910 the fact that the Liberals could not stand alone undoubtedly made the government more attentive to its commitments to radical reform. They needed Irish votes, but the Irish were a one-issue party. Since the government was committed to curbing the power of the House of Lords, it was carrying out the essential preliminary to meeting Irish aspirations. And, after the passage of the Parliament Act in 1911, it gave priority in the next three sessions to getting the Irish Home Rule Bill through the House of Commons. No other price had to be paid for Irish support. Labour co-operation was not essential to the government's survival, but it was still readily forthcoming for an administration that was passing the social welfare and trade union legislation which the Labour movement wanted. But in March 1914 when an election seemed not far off, informal overtures were made to MacDonald to bring Labour into a coalition. Throughout the period co-operation between the Liberal whips and those of the Irish Nationalists and Labour went reasonably smoothly. The lesson of the Asquith administration is that minority government presents few problems when the minor parties have nowhere else to go and when the party in power is, in any case, minded to do what the minor parties want.

1915-22

The outbreak of the First World War brought no immediate moves towards a coalition, though party warfare was suspended. However, by May 1915 the party truce was causing such strains everywhere, particularly among the Unionists, that Bonar Law proposed a coalition. Asquith agreed but kept all the major posts for Liberals, giving the Conservatives only 8 Cabinet seats out of 21. A cabinet post was also allotted to Arthur Henderson as the spokesman for the Labour members who supported the war. On this occasion the government was formed and offices allotted by direct and informal negotiation between the party leaders. The 1915-16 coalition did not, however, run smoothly. The Liberals were divided by the conscription issue and by doubts about Asquith's handling of the war, and the Conservatives were also troubled by back-bench revolts. The crisis of December 1916 which put Lloyd George in office emerged from direct negotiation between a few leading politicians, when Asquith eventually refused to have his powers curbed and the Unionists refused to continue the existing arrangement. The consequence was a much more integrated coalition, but one which, through Liberal defections, was predominantly Conservative; they had three of the five places in the inner war cabinet, while Henderson had the fourth. Whilst the Conservatives were solidly behind the coalition, Lloyd George had the support of only a minority of Liberal MPs, and Henderson's participation was endorsed by the narrowest majority in Labour's National Executive.

Parliament was uneasily managed by a Conservative Chief Whip working with a Lloyd George Liberal Chief Whip while, although there was no formal Liberal split, an official Liberal Chief Whip was still operating outside the government. None the less, so long as the war lasted, party differences within the government became less and less important; seats were exchanged in unopposed by-elections and ministerial switches were not linked to party ratios, as businessmen and other non-politicians were brought into office.

As the war came to an end, the Conservatives and the Lloyd George Liberals formed an electoral pact designed to continue the coalition in peacetime. Once again considerations arising from the electoral system were paramount; a common manifesto was drawn up and a 'coupon' issued to approved candidates. Lloyd George's prestige, helped by opposition divisions, won a landslide victory for the coupon candidates. But the composition of the House of Commons spelt the ultimate doom of Lloyd George and his coalition.

The Coalition Conservatives were in a clear majority among the MPs who took their seats and were two and a half times as numerous as the Lloyd George Liberals.

TABLE 10
General election 14 December 1918

Coalition				
Unionist	335		707	*seats*
Liberal	133		634	*participating MPs*
Labour	10	*478*		
			318	*seats needed*
Non-coalition				*for majority*
Conservative	23			
Irish Unionist	25			
Liberal	28			
Labour	63			
Irish Nationalist	7			
Others	10	*156*		
Abstentionists				
Sinn Fein	73			

(Members of Sinn Fein refused to take their seats)

Although by 1922 the Conservatives were still taking only 12 places out of 21 in the cabinet, they were necessarily the dominant partners, even though the wizardry of Lloyd George, with his flair and his non-party approach, retained the support of his senior colleagues and gave his personal stamp to the government. At the parliamentary level things were less happy. The party organizations were quite separate and there were quarrels over patronage. The Independent Conservatives and the Irish Unionists exercised an increasing influence on Tory thinking, particularly after Anti-Waste and other independents won by-elections against coalition candidates. When, inevitably, the government met with unpopularity, Lloyd George could be made the scapegoat. It became plain that the bulk of Conservatives nationally would not accept submergence into the anti-socialist fusion grouping towards which Lloyd George seemed to be manoeuvring. The vote at the Carlton Club in October 1922 (when Conservative MPs, by 187 to 88, decided to withdraw from the coalition) was, sooner or later, inevitable.

Yet the coalition did last through four years of peacetime, even though the Conservatives had the numbers to bring it down. This must be attributed partly to the standing and skill of the Prime Minister and partly to the chaos in party structure left by the war. Politicians did not know where they stood in relation to the vastly enlarged electorate. They were frightened of Bolshevism and bewildered by the confusion of the world economy. They were willing to make the compromises needed to keep the government in being. And they were enormously helped by the wartime experience of working together. Yet the coupon election, together with the latter days of the Lloyd George government and its final downfall, served to give a bad name to the idea of coalition. Baldwin and MacDonald, the dominant figures of the next dozen years, represented a moderate constitutional reaction, a return to partisanship after the unorthodox adventurism which Lloyd George, with his oddly non-party approach to coalition government, had pursued.

1923-24

The most evenly-balanced election and the most delicate problem of twentieth-century government-forming came in December 1923. Six months after becoming Prime Minister, Baldwin called an election on the issue of Tariff Reform. He reunited the Liberal party in opposition to the proposal –

and he lost his majority. The outcome was the most even three-cornered balance in British history, as Table 11 shows.

TABLE 11
General election 6 December 1923

Conservative	258	615 *seats*
Labour	191	308 *seats needed*
Liberal	151	*for majority*
Others	5	

Baldwin wanted to resign at once but he was persuaded to hold on until Parliament met in January five weeks later. Many suggestions were floated but Asquith was not prepared to join forces with the Conservatives; the Labour leaders fairly quickly decided that they would, if asked, take office alone. The Palace took soundings, not only on party feelings about who should form the government but also on current constitutional opinions about the proprieties of dissolution. However, when Baldwin was defeated on the King's Speech, MacDonald took office without any conditions from the Palace and without any understanding from the Liberal party. Labour had not yet proved that it was established as the second party in the country and it needed to advertise that it was independent from the Liberals. The inexperienced government, though possessed of less than a third of the seats in the House of Commons, managed well enough for eight months, bringing in no measures that would offend the Liberals. Its fall in October 1924 was unexpected, and indeed unnecessary, since MacDonald had no need to raise to an issue of confidence the rejection of an enquiry into the Attorney General's failure to prosecute in the Campbell case.

The main lesson of 1924 was surely that, even in circumstances far less favourable than those of 1910-14, minority government was still quite practicable. Another lesson was that a third party, with the power to bring a government down, is in an invidious position; certainly the 1924 election, which cut Labour from 191 seats to 142, hurt the Liberals even more, reducing them from 151 to a pitiful 40.

1929-31

In 1929 Labour was once again dependent on the Liberals but this time the result was clearer and Baldwin resigned as soon as the figures were known.

TABLE 12
General election 30 May 1929

Conservative	260	615 *seats*
Liberal	59	308 *seats needed*
Labour	288	*for majority*
Others	7	

MacDonald took office and again started by treating the Liberals with disdain. But in less than a year, as the government hit a rough patch, informal consultations were opened and, to conciliate the Liberals, the Ullswater Committee was appointed to look into electoral reform. MacDonald also invited Baldwin and Lloyd George to confer about the growing economic crisis; Baldwin refused, but Lloyd George agreed. When these discussions on broad policy got nowhere, the government turned back to party tactics and by September 1930 offered to legislate for the Alternative Vote. Both sides denied that this was part of a pact but there had undoubtedly been high-level discussions.

It seems that the resulting understanding was, as David Marquand put it:

> ... less a treaty than an entente, the terms of which were not wholly clear and the existence of which could be disavowed by either party if need arose.[1]

Certainly regular meetings took place during the 1930-1 session, with joint committees established to discuss particular issues. The whips worked closely together and by July 1931 MacDonald contemplated inviting Lloyd George into an alliance, with a major cabinet post. But, if a marriage of convenience was in the offing, it came to nothing since, suddenly, the government fell.

However, the understanding of 1930-1 – one authority describes it as a 'quasi-coalition' – had its price. Sir John Simon and two other Liberals resigned the whip in June 1931 and others in the Liberal party indicated their unhappiness. Closer collaboration between Liberals and Labour would have led to further explosions. The lesson of 1929-31 may be that MacDonald should have made a more comprehensive deal with Lloyd George earlier. But if such a deal had become public, the reactions in both parties might have been so vehement as to nullify the advantages to be gained from it.

1931-2

The crisis of August 1931 produced the only full-scale coalition to be formed in peacetime in this century. Faced with a run on sterling which led banking opinion to demand more cuts in government expenditure than the Labour cabinet would tolerate, MacDonald, instead of resigning, was persuaded to accept the offers of support from the Conservatives and Liberals. He formed what was intended to be a temporary National Coalition before a general election in which the parties would fight separately, with 'no coupons, no pacts'. But almost the whole of the Labour party went immediately into opposition and the other parties, after only a few weeks, decided to fight the election as a National government, with candidates of each party withdrawing in favour of whoever was the sitting tenant. The outcome was the biggest landslide in British history and, effectively, it transformed the National government into a Conservative government.

TABLE 13
General election 27 October 1931

Conservative	473	615 *seats*
National Labour	13	308 *seats needed*
Liberal National	35	*for majority*
Liberal	33	
National Government	*554*	
Independent Liberal	4	
Labour	52	
Other	5	
Opposition	*61*	

The Liberals withdrew after a year, but MacDonald remained Prime Minister until 1935; and the National label continued until 1940 with the Liberal National and National Labour parties preserving separate whips' offices and national headquarters. Yet it is hardly realistic to talk about coalition government after 1932, or to draw any lessons about how parties should work together.

The formation of the government between 21 and 24 August 1931 is, however, very important. It represents the only occasion in this century when the Palace may have played a decisive role in determining which party should form a government; it may have been the King's insistence that persuaded MacDonald to continue as Prime Minister. In the mid-August confusion, when many leading figures were away, deputy leaders of the Conservative and Liberal parties offered support to MacDonald. MacDonald found that he could not carry his cabinet on the seemingly necessary measures and, in two days of informal negotiations between the Palace and a handful of politicians, a National government emerged that was intended to be very temporary. In a less rushed situation, the party deals would have been more elaborate: as it was, they only agreed to a short seven-point statement on the measures necessary for the immediate crisis. Offices were allocated very disproportionately. It was to be 'not a coalition in the ordinary sense but a co-operation of individuals'. MacDonald, with his handful of supporters, actually kept four cabinet places out of ten for Labour. When the full government was formed after the election, National Labour retained 4 seats out of 20, although it had only 13 MPs, while the Conservatives had only 11 cabinet ministers for 473 MPs.

One special feature of the situation was provoked by the question of protection. Because of the Liberal commitment to Free Trade, policy on this issue was fudged in the joint election manifesto and later, as the government moved towards Imperial Preference, it was agreed that Liberal ministers could dissent publicly from cabinet policy. They did so for nine months until, in September 1932, they felt forced to resign over the Ottawa agreements, although the Simonites, their Liberal National colleagues, stayed on and in due course fused with the Conservatives.

One lesson to emerge from the National Government experience is that it is difficult to maintain much sense of a coalition as an instrument of compromise when one partner in the coalition is overwhelmingly stronger than the others and indeed has little real need of them.

1940-5

'The government that Winston Churchill formed on 10 May 1940 was more than a coalition. It was the only genuine National Government in British history.'[2] A.J.P.Taylor's verdict is justified by the fact that, despite some stirrings in 1942, Churchill survived without any major challenge for five years, with the support of every significant group in the House of Commons. Even the title of Leader of the Opposition was denied to James Maxton at the head of a four member ILP group from Glasgow.

Although the Labour party had given full support to the declaration of war in September 1939 they were not asked, or indeed willing, to serve under Neville Chamberlain. But in May 1940 they readily joined the administration that Winston Churchill assembled after the Norwegian débâcle. It may be significant that their decision to do so was formally endorsed by the Labour Party Conference which happened to be in session.

Despite occasional strains over the preparation of post-war social policy, the government did work as a team. In the initial War Cabinet, Labour had two places out of five; but of the 31 ministers of cabinet rank they had only 5 to the Conservatives' 25 and the Liberals' one. However some of the Conservatives were businessmen, recruited to the cabinet from outside Parliament and sitting only nominally as Conservatives. As in 1916-18, appointments were made in terms of personality not party. Inevitably the Conservatives were predominant, since they had three times as many MPs. Yet many departments tended to have a bipartisan complexion, with a Labour junior minister complementing a Conservative Secretary of State or vice versa.

It was significant that in October 1940 Churchill accepted Beaverbrook's advice to become Leader of the Conservative party, saying explicitly that he had found it a handicap, as a coalition Prime Minister dealing with the leaders of other parties, not to be a party leader himself.

The coalition ended in May 1945 after the end of the war in Europe. Churchill wanted the coalition to continue and had some support from Attlee and Bevin. But an election was long overdue and on 21 May 1945 the Labour Party Conference, egged on by Morrison, rejected the idea of staying in alliance beyond October. Thereupon the Conservatives, for tactical reasons, insisted on an immediate dissolution. The coalition government resigned. Churchill formed a precedent-setting 'caretaker' administration, drawing on the old National Government and on his wartime recruits from business and the public service. But the July election was fought essentially between Conservative, Labour and Liberal. And Labour won by a landslide.

The wartime coalition had worked better than any other coalition in British history, although it contained more disparate elements. Real compromises were reached sensibly in the interest of war-winning unity. But the spirit of co-operation could not possibly survive once that central goal was removed.

1974-9

From 1945 to 1974 single-party majorities discouraged any discussion of coalition. In the Parliament of 1950-1 Labour showed that it could govern with a majority of five, while in 1964-6 a majority of three sufficed. In neither case did the government seek to secure its position by a deal with the handful of Liberals: the legislation for which they needed more parliamentary strength mostly involved nationalization which the Liberals could hardly support.

However, 1974 brought a new era. When Mr Heath appealed to the country in February the outcome provided the first example of an indecisive election result since 1929. The Labour administration that took office then offers the

1980s the two most important precedents for governing without a majority.

TABLE 14
General election 28 Febuary 1974

Labour	301	635 *seats*
Conservative	297	318 *seats needed*
Liberal	14	*for majority*
Scottish National	7	
Plaid Cymru	2	
Northern Ireland	12	
Others	2	

When the results of the Febuary 1974 election were declared, Labour was 17 seats short of a clear majority and the Conservatives were 21 seats short. Moreover no minor party was strong enough by itself to offer security in office either to Labour or to the Conservatives. Mr Heath did not resign for three days. He sought a coalition with the Liberals and put out feelers to the Ulster Unionists. After consultation, Mr Thorpe made it plain that the Liberals would not enter a coalition: they believed that, after their great upsurge in the election, it would have been disastrous to be seen as the minor partner in a Conservative-dominated government (or in a Labour one, for that matter). An interesting aspect of the situation is that Mr Heath, in his negotiations with Mr Thorpe, insisted that the Liberals should join in a coalition and not merely give support for a minority Conservative government: one reason for this was to involve them explicitly in the budget-making process.

On 4 March, Mr Heath resigned. Mr Wilson formed a minority Labour cabinet which managed to govern for six months, largely because his opponents were not keen on an early election and therefore refrained from inflicting a serious parliamentary defeat on him until it was too late to dissolve before the summer recess. Mr Wilson had made it plain from the start that he would seek a dissolution rather than resign and advise the Queen to invite someone else to form a government. It is arguable that, if Mr Heath had resigned on 1 March without demonstrating his inability to put together a coalition, Mr Wilson would not have had so clear a claim to a dissolution if defeated on a vote of confidence, for the Crown might have waited to check whether an alternative government existed within the current House of Commons.

TABLE 15
General election 10 October 1974

Labour	319	635 *seats*
Conservative	277	318 *seats needed*
Liberal	13	*for majority*
Scottish Nationalist	11	
Plaid Cymru	3	
Northern Ireland	12	

One consequence of the February 1974 election was an aroused interest in the idea of coalition government and during the October 1974 campaign Mr Heath, in a final throw, appealed for 'a government of National Unity' bringing in the best talent without regard to party. The proposal was not fully developed; it did seem to have some attraction to the electorate – but not enough. Labour won a narrow majority over all parties.

A lead of three was sufficient to govern with and, as it proved, to pass some controversial legislation. But by-elections took their toll and by April 1976 Labour was no longer in a majority. The government continued, accepting parliamentary defeats that might, in previous times, have been considered issues of confidence.

However in March 1977, facing a vote of censure on its economic plans, the government had to act. In three days of hectic negotiations the new Labour Prime Minister, Mr Callaghan, reached a pact with the new Liberal leader, Mr Steel, by which the Liberals promised to support Labour on key votes to the end of the session in return for prior consultation on major policy initiatives, as well as for a promise that the government would go ahead with legislation for devolution and European elections (with free votes on proportional representation). The pact was continued for the 1977-8 session but the Liberals ended it with due notice at the summer recess, after the government had failed to deliver proportional representation either for Scotland or for Europe. On 28 March 1979 the Liberals helped the Conservatives to carry by one vote the no confidence motion that defeated Mr Callaghan and brought about the 3 May general election.

While it lasted, the pact worked fairly smoothly. Cabinet ministers consulted regularly – and usually harmoniously – with the Liberal spokesman. A special six-man consultative committee was established to cope with disagreements and there was a Steel-Callaghan summit as a final court of appeal. Some Labour back-benchers complained that the Liberals were far more involved in government decision-making than they were. On the other hand some Liberals, including one or two MPs, expressed worry about their party losing its identity and a special Liberal Assembly had to be called in January 1978 to endorse the pact's continuance till the summer.

The pact was a liaison of convenience. In March 1977 neither Labour nor the Liberals wanted to face an election. Mr Callaghan did not have to give away anything he really minded about to gain Liberal support. Mr Steel regarded the deal as an important step in his long-term strategy of educating the Liberals to be a party of government. But he knew that he had to detach the Liberals well before an election so that their independence was not lost and they were not too implicated in the government's failings. In retrospect he said that he would have done the same again but he regretted that the arrangement had, perforce, been rushed into so precipitately. He wrote:

> It wasn't so much a Lib-Lab pact as a Steel-Callaghan pact, accepted by our respective colleagues with widely varying degrees of enthusiasm, or lack of it ... I determined that if ever we were negotiating again ... with one of the major parties, the prior formal consent of that parliamentary party as a whole to any agreement would be essential.[3]

None the less the pact worked. For eighteen months Mr Callaghan could govern without fear of defeat, conceding points to the Liberals which he did not mind conceding and even using the pact as a defence against left-wing pressures from his own followers. In this century's twelve years of minority government it was the only period when the cabinet had a formal deal with those whose forbearance was needed to keep it in office. The Lib-Lab pact certainly has lessons for future minority governments in Britain.

*　　*　　*

When one surveys Britain's twentith century experience of coalitions, of explicit party understandings, and of minority governments, it is plain that each case has been unique, an *ad hoc* solution to a crisis. Almost all have emerged from the logic of the parliamentary situation, but almost all have been arrived at by private discussions between a very few people at the top. And the way in which they have operated in practice has depended upon the personal relationships between the leaders of the parties involved.

The style and attitudes of Callaghan and Steel in 1977-8 contrast sharply with those of MacDonald and Lloyd George in 1930-1. The Asquith-Bonar Law coalition in 1915 and the Lloyd George-Bonar Law coalition in 1916 were formed in very different ways from the Churchill-Attlee coalition in 1940. Wilson in March 1974 had much less hesitation in going it alone than MacDonald in December 1923. But, though in a minority of only 34, Wilson in 1974 had far greater problems than Asquith, in a minority of 120, faced in 1910. The situation that ended with the downfall of the Lloyd George coalition in 1922 has no analogue. And from the opposition side, the Liberals played their cards quite differently in 1924, in 1930 and in 1977.

However, even if all future crises, like all past ones, prove to be *sui generis*, one-off concatenations of circumstance, each will still be discussed in terms of principle and of precedent. In other countries where crises are more frequent, procedures have become to some extent formalized. Can we learn from what has happened in those many polities where coalition is the order of the day?

CHAPTER FOUR

Experience Abroad

———•◦•———

OUTSIDE BRITAIN coalition government is the norm not the exception. In the autumn of 1982, among European countries, only Austria and Greece had single party majority rule. Finland, Sweden, Norway, Denmark, Holland, Belgium, Luxembourg, Germany, Switzerland, Portugal, Spain and Italy had coalitions. France, although with a single-party majority, had a coalition government; Ireland, although lacking a single party majority, had a single party government.

All these countries have some variant of parliamentary government, with cabinets dependent upon command of a majority in the legislature. All have reasonably orderly arrangements for governmental continuity and for the transfer of power once it becomes impossible for those in office to carry on, whether because of an election result, or a parliamentary reverse, or an internal disagreement. Few of the procedures are established in law but many are firmly rooted in custom. Some of the devices used may be peculiar to a national political culture, but some certainly could be adapted to other systems.

It is therefore worth surveying briefly the machinery other countries have developed to cope with governmental crises before drawing a few general lessons for Britain.

Sweden

Sweden has gone further than any other country in formalizing the rules for government formation. It is also unique in taking the matter completely out of the hands of the head of state. Under the Instrument of Government of 1974, the Speaker is charged with the task which had formerly fallen to the King. He is specifically required to consult representatives of each party group and then to submit a nominee for Prime Minister to the Parliament. The name must be voted on within four days. It is approved unless more than half the full membership of the Riksdag vote against − in other words, abstentions effectively count as votes in favour and the forming of a minority government is thus facilitated. If four nominees are each rejected in turn, there have to be new elections.

One notable disadvantage of this system lies in the fact that the Speaker is elected anew in each parliament − but the start of a parliament is the moment when a problem of government-formation is most likely. So far the outgoing Speaker has been re-elected but there can be no guarantee against the difficulties of the situation being exacerbated by the need first to settle on a Speaker.

On each occasion since 1974 the Speaker, after consulting the parties, has not only named a candidate for Prime Minister; he has also indicated which parties should compose the prospective government. There has as yet been no serious difficulty, but some Swedes have expressed anxiety about the power a Speaker might exercise if more complicated crises were to arise. There is more fear of a transient Speaker overreaching himself than of a permanent monarch doing so, since the latter has perhaps a much greater lasting interest in avoiding any suspicion of partisanship.

Until 1976 Sweden had had 44 years of Social Democratic rule with, for 29 out of those 44 years, a single-party government. After that it had four governments, all of them coalitions among the three 'bourgeois' parties, some, but not all, commanding a joint majority in the Riksdag. Coalition government worked for six years until the 1982 election returned the Socialists to power. Although Sweden has a very co-operative style of politics, her party divisions are clear enough: in practice the government has to be either Socialist or based on an alliance of the bourgeois parties – something that has never proved very difficult to achieve. The four-day time-limit helped the bourgeois parties to settle their differences speedily. The strict rules of the 1974 constitution did solve problems well enough in the six-year interregnum of 1976-82 between periods of Socialist domination.

Norway

The King in Norway is formally charged by the constitution with choosing the Prime Minister and cabinet. In practice he normally acts on the advice of the outgoing Prime Minister. Government crises have been relatively swiftly solved by inter-party negotiation. Since 1963 the King has asked the Speaker to act as *informateur* or honest broker.

During the arguments over entry to the European Community, Norwegians found it impossible to agree on a coalition and thus in 1971 and 1972, the country had minority governments, each of which lasted a year. Norway, alone among the countries considered here, has fixed-term parliaments with no possibility of dissolution.

In calling on a *formateur* to see if he can assemble a practicable government, the King has little discretion. He has acted on the advice of the outgoing Prime Minister or the *informateur*. In the conciliatory politics of Norway, crises have not lasted long: they have been settled by direct negotiation between party leaders rather than through any formal conference. But there have often been problems between the bourgeois parties, and the premiership has not always gone to the largest party.

Denmark

Denmark has had more crises, and more difficulty in solving them, than the other Scandinavian countries. The Danish constitution like the Norwegian requires the sovereign to appoint and dismiss the Prime Minister and the other ministers. In practice, governments hold office subject to Parliament although they do not need a vote of confidence for their installation (which makes it easier to have minority governments).

When there is a crisis, the Sovereign's secretary (a personal appointee of the Crown) usually consults all the party leaders in turn and makes a recommendation. But on some occasions, an *informateur* has been appointed from among the senior politicians in the Folketing, to suggest a leader and a party composition for the next cabinet.

Since it has often been impossible for enough parties to agree to make up a majority government, minority governments have been common, and it has not been obvious which alternative would have the best chance of survival. An ultimate decision does rest with the monarch. But the monarch's decisions have not in fact caused serious controversy at any time in the last 60 years.

Unlike Norway, the Danish Prime Minister can always ask for a dissolution, although there is an informal rule that he will not do so until six months have elapsed since the last election.

The reason why government-formation has become so complicated in Denmark lies in the recent multiplication of parties and the consequent collapse of the simple assumption, still valid in Norway and Sweden, that the choice lies between a basically socialist government and a coalition of the bourgeois parties.

Party splits and the emergence of anti-system groups, like Mogens Glistrup's anti-tax Progress Party, have enormously increased the possible permutations and the difficulties. The Queen has often had to call a conference of all parties to search for a solution. The answer can lie in the lowest common denominator. From 1973-5 Denmark was ruled by a single-party minority cabinet, drawn from the Venstre party which commanded only 22 out of the 119 MPs. The fact that this government could survive so long, and be followed by a minority Labour cabinet which lasted two years, is a tribute to the relaxed style of Danish politics.

Belgium

Belgium has institutionalized, more than other countries, the idea of an *informateur* and a *formateur*. The King, often described as the only Belgian in a country divided into Flemings and Walloons, has a positive, but so far uncriticized, role. When a crisis occurs (as it has done with increasing frequency over the last decade), he consults all the party leaders, as well as major figures from industry and the trade unions, and then appoints a senior politician to act as *informateur*. The *informateur* spends up to a week consulting all parties before recommending a *formateur* or possible Prime Minister and, usually, specifying the party composition of the government. The *formateur* then spends up to three weeks negotiating with a team from each party on the policies the government would follow. Once this is settled, it only takes a few days to allocate portfolios; approval is then sought from the relevant party organizations before Parliament is asked for a vote of confidence, which is usually forthcoming. The first nominated *formateur* often fails in his negotiations and up to four candidates have been tried before success has been achieved.

The process of government-forming has become more

difficult in Belgium as a result of the growing linguistic gap which has bifurcated each party into separate Flemish and Walloon groupings. It has also become more difficult because of the growing role played by representatives of the mass parties in the negotiations: they are less pliable, or less realistic, than the parliamentarians.

It is said that all major policy-making in Belgium takes place during government crises. The deal worked out then acts as a fairly immutable blueprint for all cabinet decisions until the next crisis changes the situation once more.

Holland

The Dutch have the most extreme form of proportional representation and the greatest number of parliamentary parties of any Western democracy. They also have the most protracted of governmental crises. But oddly enough, the duration of the crises is not due to the proliferation of very small parties (which results from an electoral system where 1 per cent of the vote is enough to secure representation). It turns on the obduracy of the three large parties, two of which must normally combine for a government to be formed. The Queen has said she 'merely acts as postman', and on the whole, governmental crises are conducted in the party arena, as the leaders fight over issues and offices. An *informateur* usually distances the head of state from the preliminary bargaining, and then the recommended Prime Minister has to see if he can piece together a coalition. Meanwhile, the outgoing government carries on as a 'caretaker' administration, often for months.

The German Federal Republic

West Germany may offer the most relevant example of coalition-making for Britain. She has had coalitions ever since 1949 and only three parties in Parliament from

1961-83. Each of the parties has, at some time, partnered the other in government.

Most of the coalitions have been formed, *de facto*, in advance of an election and the voters have known the likely consequence of their votes. After an election, it has taken ten days or so to agree on policy and then to agree on the share-out of offices. Once the parties have decided to try to form a coalition they have never failed because of disputes over the government programme or the distribution of portfolios. And the coalitions which have been formed have been very enduring. They have, in the majority of cases, lasted for a full parliament.

One source of stability lies in the constitutional rule that a German Chancellor can be ousted only by a 'constructive vote of no confidence' naming an alternative Chancellor. Another lies in the 5 per cent threshold which has kept independents and minor parties out of the Bundestag. The key to the German situation has lain with the Free Democrats, who, although at times only just above the 5 per cent threshold, have held the balance of power for twenty years. Before 1966 they sided with the Christian Democrats; between 1969 and 1982 they supported the Social Democrats; then they reverted to their earlier partnership with the right. In cabinet they have had a share of ministries roughly proportionate in number to their parliamentary strength. Their influence may have been somewhat disproportionate (partly because of their near-monopoly of the Economics and Agriculture portfolios), yet it cannot be said that they have dominated politics or, by threatening to change sides, have forced all governments to toe their line. However in 1982 they did switch sides in mid-Parliament, voting Schmidt and the Social Democrats out, and Kohl and the Christian Democrats in. Schmidt could not muster the majority in the Bundestag needed to meet the conditions for dissolution so that the issue could be put to the country. A gap in the Constitution makes dissolution singularly difficult; it is necessary for a government desiring to dissolve to arrange for its own defeat on a motion of confidence, and to convince the Federal President that there is no alternative government available in the current Bundestag.

West Germany has had stable government for a generation, but she may have been lucky. In 1969 the *non-ministrable* neo-Nazi party (NPD) got almost 5 per cent of the vote and the highly *ministrable* Free Democratic Party almost fell below that mark, a double escape from a situation which would have made orderly government difficult.[1] The relatively *non-ministrable* ecologists, the Greens, have already ousted the FDP as the third party in several Land elections and they could do so federally. German coalition politics would have been very different if, in the last quarter-century, there had been more than three parties in the Bundestag, or if any of them had been *non-ministrable* The three-party system has been described as a two-and-a-half party system. If it becomes a two-and-two-halves party system, it may become much more unstable. But the main lesson West Germany can give Britain does perhaps lie in the virtue of constitutional rules which require the Bundestag to endorse a Chancellor before he takes office and, in most circumstances, to lend their co-operation if there is to be a premature dissolution.

Italy

Among the countries of Europe, Italy has the most complex of party systems and the most short-lived of governments. Her solutions to the problems of cabinet-forming are perhaps the least likely to be relevant to Britain. But the President of Italy probably plays a more positive role than any other head of state discussed in this chapter.[2] He has to decide whether to press the retiring Prime Minister to try again or, alternatively, he has to select from among several possible candidates out of a single party. In seeking to form a government a potential Prime Minister has to negotiate with three or four small parties and with factions within the larger parties. Although the ritual dance of government crisis has been performed more often in Italy than in any other country over the last 30 years, the system still seems to work more unpredictably.

Israel

Israel, like the Netherlands, has an almost perfectly proportional electoral system. One per cent of the votes secures a seat in the 120-member Knesset which has never contained fewer than nine parties. But so far the President of Israel has had little opportunity to exercise influence. For 30 years the leader of Mapai, the largest party, always formed the government. Since 1977 the leader of Likud, the largest party on the other side, has provided the Prime Minister. Government-forming has not been a swift process. It is subject to a 119-day limit on negotiations and has often taken 7 or 8 weeks. There are two notable features in the negotiations. New cabinet offices are frequently created to balance off minority-party claims to full involvement in the administration. And the final coalition deal is presented in the form of a detailed public document.

Ireland

The Irish political system derives in most respects from Britain. However Ireland has had proportional representation since the establishment of the constitution in 1922. For most of her history she has had single party Fianna Fail governments, usually commanding a clear majority in the Dail. When, in 1948, she first acquired a coalition, there was an ill-fated attempt to break away from the traditions of collective responsibility. But her subsequent coalitions in 1954 and 1973 represented fairly close alliances between the anti-Fianna Fail parties. In each case the deals were made after, not before the election, but in each case they lasted. In 1981-2, for the first time in 60 years of proportional representation, Ireland suffered the caricature ills of a narrowly balanced system lacking a clear majority. The Fine Gael/Labour government of Garret FitzGerald fell in February after seven months in office because of the votes of the handful of independent deputies. The same happened in November to the Fianna Fail government of Charles Haughey.

In Ireland the electoral system and deep-rooted voting habits have meant that only Fianna Fail could hope to form a goverment on its own. Whatever their differences, Fine Gael and Labour have been condemned to govern together if they were to govern at all. Proportional representation, coupled with stable voting patterns, in this case have simplified coalition choices by leaving no alternative combination – and no prospect of another election producing an alternative.

Canada

Canada has had a clear majority in every election but one from 1867 to 1953. But, through chance and the rise of third parties, 6 of the 10 elections in the last 25 years have failed to produce a definite outcome. These have produced not coalitions but minority governments – and on only one occasion has there been even a semblance of an understanding between the government and a minor party. The six minority governments since 1957 have on average lasted two years and only one fell within twelve months. Canada has a parliamentary system very much based on the British model, but she is a federal country, where many controversial issues are settled at the provincial level; she is also, in many ways, a comparatively non-ideological country and relatively few questions arise which divide the parties irrevocably. None the less, as the anglicised Canadian, R.T.McKenzie, delighted to point out, his native country offers a standing refutation to any assumption that, within the Westminster model, a parliamentary majority is necessary to good government. After each general election, the leader of the largest party in the Canadian House of Commons has been asked to form a cabinet and has governed until defeated on an issue of confidence. He has then dissolved – and on five of the six occasions, the minority Prime Minister has emerged the winner from the ensuing contest.

Australia

Australia has had coalition government for 30 out of the last 33 years. But, although the Liberal Party/National Country Party's coalition has been based on genuinely separate parties, at times pursuing separate goals, Australia has had an essentially two-party system – Labor and anti-Labor. The association between the Liberal party and the Country party has been facilitated by the electoral system. The Alternative Vote allows them to contest disputed seats without handing them over to Labor on a split vote. The two parties, representing different economic interests, have been bound to work together, because both were much more fundamentally opposed to Labor than to each other and neither could normally hope for a majority on its own. They have shared out ministerial offices strictly in proportion to their parliamentary strength, but they have always fought elections as two separate parties with separate platforms, not as a government. The Liberals have necessarily been the senior partner, since the Australian electorate is predominantly urban and the Country party has little chance in urban seats, but they have submitted to Country party pressure on tariffs and agricultural policy. Each partner has been master of its own segment of cabinet representation.

India

India, in her 35 years of independence, has had 33 years of rule by the Congress party alone. Her one experience of coalition government came in 1977 from a pre-election pact between almost all the opposition parties, whose candidates trounced Mrs Gandhi's supporters in straight fights. But the coalition fell apart very quickly because of its disparate nature and its failure to work out in advance a comprehensive agreement on policy. It provides the extreme example of a coalition with an essentially negative *raison d'etre*. The opposition groupings were agreed on getting rid of Mrs Gandhi and her 'emergency' but they lacked any basic understanding of what they wanted to do with power if they got it.

*   *   *

What lessons can be drawn from this catalogue of foreign experience?

1 The role of the head of state has been very limited. It has seldom been the subject of controversy, even in countries like Italy and Belgium where difficult decisions have sometimes been necessary. All sides recognize the need for an umpire and that it is in the general interest to support his decisions. So perhaps it does not matter too much who is umpire, since, in the last resort, he has to produce an answer which is acceptable to the elected chamber.

2 'Caretaker' adminstrations, usually the outgoing cabinet, can manage affairs for long periods while a new government is being formed. In most countries crises are settled in a few days but in Belgium and Italy they have lasted for several weeks and in Holland for several months. So perhaps there is no need to rush to a decision on the day the election result becomes known.

3 The device of appointing an *informateur* has been increasingly used in Scandinavia and the Low Countries. Usually the *informateur* is a senior parliamentarian, who for some reason is not considered a potential *formateur*. His role, as honest broker, charged with suggesting where an answer may be found, has usually been non-controversial. But perhaps, in a complicated situation, an *informateur* could save the head of state from being seen as the prime instigator of a particular solution to a crisis.

4 In countries with few parties, the components of a coalition may be agreed, and indeed publicized, in advance of an election. But the details of any deal always await an exact knowledge of the parliamentary arithmetic. Coalition-forming can be an infinitely complex process and perhaps parties should always beware of premature contracts.

5 Offices have normally been distributed in proportion to parliamentary strength. But offices are not equal in import-ance and parties often care more about which portfolios they gain rather than how many. Parties with sectional interests want to control particular departments and the prestige offices; those dealing with finance and foreign affairs, tend to be the main bones of contention. Yet it seems that difficulties in government-forming have arisen more often over policy than over the distribution of offices. It is easier to agree on who gets what than on what shall be done, because, except for the one or two people immediately involved, the mass of politicians care more about the stance they have got to defend than about the exact personnel of government.

6 Most major decisions by coalition governments are made in the process of government-forming rather than during the life of the government. This is a major reason why crises last so long: the delay can occur because really important issues are being settled and not because of petty haggling. But the success of a coalition deal probably lies ultimately in its flexibility, in its capacity to allow unforeseen problems to be settled without a break-up.

7 Most coalitions are minimal in size, containing only just enough parties to command a majority. Broader coalitions are harder to form; moreover the spoils in terms of policies and posts have to be shared between more partners.

8 Minority governments have been tried in almost every country and have often lasted for a considerable time. Sometimes (but by no means always) there is an explicit deal by which other parties agree not to bring them down.

9 The durability of coalitions is influenced by whether Parliament has a fixed term, either legally or through established custom. The possibility of asking for a dissolution can be a weapon in the hands of a threatened government. On the other hand, the fact that there cannot be a dissolution may encourage dissatisfied coalition partners to bring about a crisis, both in the knowledge that they are indispensable to any government drawn from the current Parliament, and in the hope that they would do better from a new deal. However, in countries where dissolutions are possible, parties have been slow to invoke them. Since 1960, Greece (1963-4), Ireland (1981-2), Portugal (1979-80), Japan (1979-80) and Canada (1979-80) are the only democracies, apart from Britain (1974) to have two general elections within twelve months.

10 A major element conditioning the flexibility of negotiations lies in the number of *non-ministrables* in Parliament, groupings of the far left or the far right, or religious or regional extremists, who would be totally unacceptable in any government, even if they were willing to take part.

11 The role of the parliamentary and extra-parliamentary parties varies widely. In Belgium, bringing into negotiating teams non-parliamentary figures is said to have complicated and slowed Cabinet-forming since such people are less versed in the art of compromise. But the need to get explicit mass party endorsement of a deal before it is completed may inevitably tie the hands of negotiators.

12 Deals are sometimes open, sometimes secret. But they seldom reach very far into the future. They usually break down because some unforeseen issue arises to divide the coalition partners.

This chapter has been concerned with actual practice in countries with experience of coalition government. There is, of course, also a large body of more general academic theorizing about coalitions. Much of it stems from formal game-theory. The 'prisoner's dilemma', which discusses the optimum tactics for a wholly self-interested person in a situation where his interests may be maximized by a degree of co-operation with others, has provoked a large body of literature. But most of the formal work in this area is based on rigorous but very simplified assumptions about the actors and the goals involved. Political parties, with a past tradition and a loyal clientele, are not free agents: they are subject to complex constraints; for example, they have to bear in mind long-term considerations, such as how their current actions will affect their image and their stance in the next round – or the next round but three. They cannot follow the simple dictates of self-interest assumed in most game-theory. Those who have tried to apply the theories to the actual world have, on the whole, retreated in dismay. General laws perversely refuse to apply to particular polities. The exceptions are so numerous that every generalization tends, for all practical purposes, to dissolve. Denmark refutes Italy; Holland refutes Israel. Indeed Denmark often refutes Denmark, and Holland refutes Holland, as new solutions emerge from seemingly similar situations.

One example may suffice. On *a priori* grounds it is widely

argued that the solution found will tend to be the 'minimum winning coalition', a combination of parties that just supplies a working majority.[3] The spoils of office, in jobs and in policy, would thus be shared among the fewest partners. But no country accustomed to coalition government has consistently followed that pattern. Repeatedly, those forming coalitions have chosen to ally with a party that was not the smallest of those that could give them a majority, or have included in the government extra parties over and above the minimum needed.

At the end of one of the best books on coalitions, Eric Browne, looking at the several theoretical explanations of coalitional behaviour, based on axiomatic structures describing the behaviour of rational actors, and the tests of those explanations in real political settings, concludes:

> It is fair to say that the results of these tests to date have been disappointing, either demonstrating little support for theoretical propositions or leading to no clear conclusion.[4]

But, if abstract theory is so disappointing, foreign experience, although often special to a particular society and incapable of export, may contain lessons and devices which might helpfully be translated into the British scene.

CHAPTER FIVE

Forming a Government

THE PAST EXPERIENCE of Britain and the examples from abroad offer only limited guidance on what should or would happen the next time that there is no majority in Parliament. The situations that may arise in the 1980s and 1990s will probably not parallel those of the 1920s, still less the 1850s. And the reactions of British politicians to this new situation will doubtless fail to mirror closely those of their continental counterparts.

Let us consider some of the posibilities, focussing on post-election situations. A Parliament without a one-party majority, although it may come after by-election losses or a party split, is most likely to arise from a general election. Table 16 sets out three possible results. They are chosen, not because they are the three most probable outcomes – they are not especially likely, although none of them is wholly implausible – but because they illustrate most of the main problems. Scenario A envisages a three-way split, with all the main groupings more or less equal and able to bargain on level terms: December 1923 offers the closest parallel to this. Scenario B envisages two dominant parties, either of which could be put into office by a third, but much smaller, party: May 1929 offers the closest parallel to this. Scenario C envisages a more complex situation where at least three parties would have to co-operate to provide a majority (unless the two big opposing parties could sink their differences): March 1974 offers the closest parallel to this. It is not self-evident who would form the government in any of these situations. Each would leave all the principal actors with dilemmas about what constituted their rights and their duties, and about where their self-interest lay. Few of these dilemmas can be categorically resolved. This chapter sets out some basic questions and some of the contradictory answers that are currently available.

In the very broadest terms, of course, there is complete consensus. Few would challenge a formulation such as this:

> When an election fails to produce a clear result, it is open to the incumbent Prime Minister to resign at once or to continue in office until defeated in Parliament. If he resigns, the Queen will ask someone else to form a government and present a Queen's Speech to Parliament. If the government, old or new, is defeated on an amendment to the Queen's Speech, the Prime Minister will either resign or ask for a dissolution.

But that statement begs a very large number of questions. To give three examples out of many: What should guide the Prime Minister in deciding whether to soldier on or not? What should guide the Queen in deciding for whom she should send in his place? Can any defeated Prime Minister count on a request for dissolution being granted automatically? Behind these questions is a larger issue. Are the rules which have guided or which would guide the leading actors in such a crisis, the best that could be devised for Britain in the 1980s? Should new conventions be developed? Should new umpires be found?

In most multi-party situations the final outcome of the crisis may be clear from the outset. Public opinion polls will have given some warning of the possible election result and questioning during the campaign will have clarified some party attitudes towards various types of coalition. There may already have been private party deals. Yet, in one sense, polling day wipes the slate clean. A new deal is needed once

TABLE 16
Variations on a hung parliament

Scenario A   Three equal groupings

			Seats	Share of vote
Conservative			215	32%
Labour			210	27%
Liberal	110	Alliance	200	34%
SDP	90			
NI Orange	12			
NI Green	5			
Scot Nat	3	Others	25	7%
Welsh Nat	2			
Independent	3			
Total			650	100%

Scenario B   Two parties needed for a majority

			Seats	Share of vote
Conservative			290	35%
Labour			300	34%
Liberal	20	Alliance	35	23%
SDP	25			
NI Orange	12			
NI Green	5			
Scot Nat	3	Others	25	8%
Welsh Nat	2			
Independent	3			
Total			650	100%

Scenario C   Two strong parties and one weak party (More than two parties needed for a majority)

			Seats	Share of vote
Conservative			280	35%
Labour			285	33%
Liberal	20	Alliance	35	22%
SDP	15			
NI Orange	12			
NI Green	5			
Scot Nat	8	Others	50	10%
Welsh Nat	2			
Independent	23			
Total			650	100%

These three scenarios are based on the assumption that the 1982 redistribution proposals of the Boundary Commissioners have taken effect and that there has been a broadly uniform swing from the votes cast in 1979.

prior suppositions about the outcome have become established facts. Party leaders and parties are reluctant to tie themselves down on what they would do in hypothetical situations. During a campaign parties tend to declare their faith in complete victory: they believe it would be counter-productive to admit to any lesser expectation and therefore they cannot realistically discuss how they would react in a deadlock situation; they cannot even go very far in reaching private deals, since a leak at the climax of the campaign could be very costly in votes.

But even if deals cannot be completed before the election, they may present little difficulty afterwards. If, as in

Scenario A, no party has a majority but any two groups out of three can combine to provide one, the permutations are limited. If one party, say Labour, announces that it will not take part in any coalition, then the choice is reduced to either a Conservative/Alliance coalition or a minority government. It is fairly certain that a few days of inter-party bargaining would produce a solution, without any prompting from the Palace and without any constitutional hassles.

But this book is designed to tackle the more complicated dilemmas that may well arise when a simple arrangement between well-disposed parties is not practicable. Let us consider sixteen questions that could each, at some point in the coming decades, suddenly become the subject of much agitation and many columns of print.

1 After an election in which the government has lost its majority, what determines the Prime Minister on whether to hang on or resign at once? There can be no simple answer. So long as the Prime Minister sees a serious chance of assembling enough support to survive any vote on the Queen's Speech, resignation is unlikely. But to be perceived as clinging to office after losing an election may have adverse effects on public opinion. It might be tactically wiser to force the other side, or sides, to demonstrate that they cannot form an administration. Consider 1974. If Mr Heath's government had resigned at once on Friday 1 March, 1974 and Mr Wilson had then been defeated in the division lobbies, Mr Heath would have had some claim to be given another chance. His demonstrated failure to make a deal with the Liberals over the weekend of 3 March cleared the way for Mr Wilson to govern with a claim to a dissolution on demand.

After an election the basic consideration facing the incumbent Prime Minister must lie in the parliamentary arithmetic. Has he got the numbers? Can he assemble them? If the answers are 'no' he will be well advised to go quickly and graciously. If the answers are 'yes', he should plainly stay on. If the answer is indeterminate, there is nothing wrong in waiting while the situation gets clarified.

Apart from December 1923, Britain has never had a succession crisis that has lasted more than a few days. The Prime Minister of a defeated government has resigned as soon as the results were known and a new and lasting government has been formed at once. It has been a very swift process, completed in a matter of hours. Politicians and the public are habituated to expect immediate action. The removal vans arrive at Downing Street less than twenty-four hours from the close of poll. Mr Heath was criticized in 1974 for waiting for three days to acknowledge that he could no longer run the government. Although a miners' strike was in progress and there was some degree of national crisis, there was no necessity for extreme haste; the idea that decisions must be instantly arrived at can be pernicious. Normally cabinets face few controversial decisions that have to be taken immediately. The Netherlands provide an object lesson: the orderly way in which government has continued during cabinet-forming, in that most orderly of countries, suggests that it is normally possible to pause for weeks, or even months, while the right answer is found. It is also worth noting the ten-week transition between election and presidential inauguration in the United States and, in parliamentary systems, the two-week pause in Ireland and the six-week pause in Spain before, in 1982, victor took over from vanquished.

None the less the media will huddle around the Prime Minister and all other leading politicians, demanding their intentions and their expectations and seeking to uncover each private contact or negotiation. Just as they did during the Falklands invasion, television producers will invoke every kind of expert to speculate on what might happen and on what should happen. Such pressures will put a very heavy premium on speedy action. One cannot envisage a Prime Minister today being allowed, like Baldwin in December 1923, to wait for six weeks for the dust to settle. The law of anticipated reactions works much faster nowadays. The logic of what must happen is driven home from every quarter. The future becomes the present more swiftly than it did a generation ago. But the rush to judgement should probably be resisted. Quicker decisions are often worse decisions. If, in fact, it is not clear what combinations, based on what understandings, have the best chance of commanding a Commons' majority that will last for a reasonable period of time, politicians may be well advised to go slow and to brief editors and reporters that the whole business will not be settled for a while.

2 If the crisis takes time, who minds the shop?

Normally Parliament meets a week after an election and its first few days are occupied with choosing a Speaker and swearing in the members. Even in ordinary times, two weeks elapse before a Queen's Speech is presented to the House of Commons.

It is, however, worth stressing that the routines of government are always suspended for the three weeks of the election campaign. Decision-making is reduced to a minimum once Parliament is dissolved. The pause can indeed be substantially longer. In 1979, after defeat on the confidence vote of 28 March, Mr Callaghan's government continued on a 'caretaker' basis until the election on 3 May. The Chancellor of the Exchequer Mr Healey, presented an uncontroversial care and maintenance Budget on 13 April, drawn up after consultation with the Shadow Chancellor, Sir Geoffrey Howe. The five weeks when routine affairs were managed by civil servants, with occasional consultations with campaigning ministers, could easily have been extended for two or three weeks more if the election had produced an indeterminate result. There is no imperative necessity for the Prime Minister to resign on the day after the election.

There will, of course, be a danger of dispute over the propriety of a 'caretaker' administration in the weeks after an election by a government that, it may widely be thought, has lost its mandate. But the analogy of April 1979 can be cited as evidence that it is possible for a lame-duck administration, in consultation with the other parties, to take a few decisions that cannot wait. Half a century ago, Sir Ivor Jennings wrote firmly, 'It is essential to the parliamentary system that a Cabinet should be formed, and the Cabinet must remain until its successors have been appointed.'[1]

3 Who does the Prime Minister consult about whether or when to resign?

In this century the pre-eminence of the Prime Minister over his colleagues has become more and more accepted. Prime Ministers have often acted without any consultation, not only in hiring and firing senior colleagues but also in recommending dissolutions and in resigning. It may be prudent for a Prime Minister to involve his colleagues in such decisions, partly because they may have wise advice to offer and partly in order to spread the blame if the outcome is not what was intended. Harold Wilson consulted few people in March 1966, but in May 1970, once he had decided that the time was ripe, he involved the whole cabinet in the decision to dissolve. It is, however, plain that no constitutional Prime Minister acted unilaterally in resigning after an election setback. As we see in later discussions, the current primacy of the Prime Minister may be thought undesirable. There may be a need, particularly in coalition and minority situations, for new and limiting conventions to be established: but these will never prevent an individual from choosing to give up office whenever he feels he should, even though in a Prime Minister's case, the decision must involve putting every other minister's office on the block.

4 While the crisis is in progress, where may the Queen turn for advice?   Everything done by the state is done in the name of the Crown. But in practice the Palace has been depoliticized over the last two centuries by the principle that the sovereign always acts on the advice of ministers. However, we are here envisaging a situation in which there are no ministers, or only ministers who have been repudiated by the electorate or by the House of Commons. At such a time there may be no one in a position to give advice to the monarch which may seem legitimate.

It is possible to question whether, in a crisis, it is desirable for decisions over appointments and dissolutions to be thrust on the sovereign. But, while there may be problems about the Queen trying to act as a neutral umpire, there could be even greater problems if she were obliged, in default of anyone else, to act on the advice of a lame-duck Prime Minister. It would be widely seen as outrageous if, in an essentially adversarial situation, the umpire had to act on the advice of one of the protagonists. The sovereign has very seldom faced a constitutional dilemma in this century without having a Prime Minister to offer guidance that was virtually mandatory. But if the development of multi-party politics makes a vacuum a much more frequent occurrence, it may be desirable to establish new conventions which renders absolutely clear the principles that are guiding the monarch's decisions.

However, the Queen is not on her own. She does have a Private Secretary to help her in an informal but very professional way. The sovereign's secretary has long been a person of seniority and great political experience, a man who has met all the leading politicians, socially as well as officially, and who has read and consulted widely among constitutional experts. There is no doubt that the Palace provides the sovereign with a very sophisticated infrastructure of guidance on constitutional principle and on current politics. But neutrality is a subtle concept. Everyone has his prejudices and the left could easily be tempted to argue that the Queen's advisers are upper-class, establishment figures, much more attuned to Conservative than to Labour thinking.[2]

On the other hand, the Queen and her advisers have an overwhelming interest in being seen to act as impartially and uncontroversially as possible. But what does that involve or preclude? Who may the Private Secretary speak to? Must his be only a listening role? Can he pass on messages? Can he suggest solutions?

There is no doubt that anyone associated with the Palace has to exercise extreme discretion. Listening is relatively easy: in a crisis the Palace will receive by letter and by telephone plenty of information and plenty of ideas on what should be done. Such gratuitous advice can readily be sorted into the sensible and the irrelevant. But the positive search for guidance is more delicate. At an informal level, would it be proper for the Private Secretary to telephone a party leader to seek his views on the next course of action? Or, to venture further, would it be proper for the Private Secretary to solicit views from ex-Prime Ministers or other elder statesman? More adventurously still, would it be proper for the Private Secretary to contact dissident but significant figures among active politicians who might differ from their party leaders?

However complete the assurances of discretion, the Private Secretary must be ultra-careful. Even if there are no leaks, hardened politicians can be influenced by pique or by paranoia; they can wreck a negotiation because they were not consulted when others were; they can be sensitive, too, about who was consulted first.

On the whole, therefore, informal consultations by Palace officials may be minimal. Perhaps they can count on enough information flowing towards them spontaneously, publicly through the saturation coverage of television, radio and the press, and privately through the initiative of most of the leading actors on the scene. It would be easy to indicate that such enterprise would be not unwelcome.[3]

Moreover, it is possible to be too worried about the dangers. If the Private Secretary makes it plain that he is consulting every party leader, he can probe quite widely. Without taking any positive initiative or putting forward proposals in his own right, he can explore all sorts of possibilities under suitable forms of words. 'What did you think of that suggestion in *The Times?*.' 'Could you comment on the proposition in Mr X's speech?' ''It has been put to me that one solution would be. . .' The people he is talking to may make some deductions from the thrust of his questions but, like a skilled industrial arbitrator, he can probably leave little room for charges of bias. In choosing the areas to probe he will be guided by the likelihood that partisan sounding proposals will seldom be useful and useful proposals will seldom sound partisan.

However, in addition to any private contacts, there must also be a formal show of consultation. Unrecorded communications with the Private Secretary and others around the Palace are one thing; official visits to the Queen are another. In 1957 the Queen saw Lord Salisbury as the senior peer in the cabinet, and Sir Winston Churchill as the only Conservative ex-Prime Minister, before summoning Mr Macmillan to form a government. In 1963 she visited Mr Macmillan in hospital to hear his report on the whips' poll of MPs and on other Conservative soundings.

In countries with more complex party systems, there can be a formal routine when a crisis occurs. Belgium provides a notable example, as Chapter 4 recorded. The head of state may see briefly and in turn the leaders of each party represented in the legislature. (The sequence is usually decided by the size of the party's representation.) In British terms, that could raise problems. Consider the multi-party situation set out in Scenario C at the beginning of this chapter. Would the Queen see in turn the leaders of both the Liberal party and the SDP, or only the one who had already been declared the leader of the Alliance? Would she see the leader of a two-member Plaid Cymru as well as someone from each of the separate Ulster factions? It would doubtless be politic to err on the side of inclusiveness in such situations; however, the Westminster world might not think it unreasonable if a line were drawn at, say, groupings of fewer than three.

To see and to listen is simple. To decide on action is more complicated. It is not possible to legislate in advance for all hypothetical situations. But it may be possible to signal, well in advance of any crisis, the routines that will be followed, in order that the number of people offended, either by exclusion or by their position in the rank-ordering of consultations, will be as few as possible.[4]

Routine public consultations may be a necessary show, a demonstration that justice is being seen to be done. But they may also be of substantive importance. In a knife-edge situation it is essential that those at the centre should have the maximum information about the views of everyone involved. However vigilant the media are in their reports (which are doubtless studied more searchingly at the Palace than anywhere else), the infinitely discreet decision-makers need to know more, and, with more certainty, about the positions of the party leaders than they can ever learn through indirect and public sources. What the spokesman for the Scottish Nationalists or the Ulster Unionists may convey privately to the Queen and her Private Secretary will not be identical to what they say to the political editor of the

Scotsman or the *Belfast Telegraph.* In the early stages of a crisis the Palace will listen: it will not talk. But the remit given to a *formateur* may be substantially influenced by the judgements developed at the Palace after hearing the views of those who might matter, in minor as well as in major parties.

5 Should the whole matter be removed from the Sovereign's hands? In a recent article Tony Benn suggested that:

> The best way to avoid [drawing the monarchy into the heart of political debate] would be to ... transfer the power of dissolution and the power to ask a person to form a government ... to the Speaker of the House of Commons.[5]

Mr Benn could point out that this was precisely what was done by the 1974 Constitution in Sweden. But such a scheme, it must also be realized, might actually raise more problems than it solves.

The arguments for making a change are two-edged. They can be put forward in a pro-monarchical or an anti-monarchical spirit. One can argue sympathetically that to remove the government-choosing function from the Queen would save her from potential involvement in politics. In delicate negotiations, the exact sequence of who is called when, and on what conditions, may be regarded as crucial; at some points, a decision in any direction will be bound to excite partisan criticism. Should the Queen be spared this hazard? Could not the head of state, the symbol of national unity, be freed from any liability of taking sides in partisan disputes – or even of appearing to do so?

Mr Benn's argument is that any decision which is in essence political must be controversial. If the sovereign makes a decision (perhaps entirely correctly) that partisans can construe as anti-Labour or anti-working class (or indeed anti-Tory), that decision necessarily becomes a centre of dispute, and the sovereign's standing and national authority is thereby reduced. The sovereign, so this argument runs, can only be sovereign as long as the sovereignty is never exercised in a way that can provoke controversy.

This is a strong and far-reaching argument. But it is worth pointing out that the only serious disputes about the exercise of royal or quasi-royal power under the Westminster model have occurred in vice-regal situations – Lord Byng in Canada in 1925, Sir Philip Game in New South Wales in 1932, Sir Patrick Duncan in South Africa in 1939, the Oni of Ife in Western Nigeria in 1962 and Sir John Kerr in Australia in 1975. In Britain, the sovereign's decisions have provoked little criticism, except for some Labour suspicions about the minimal intervention in 1931. In Europe, where there have been many fraught situations, the sovereigns in Norway, Denmark, Holland and Belgium have, to an extraordinary degree, emerged as uncriticized and accepted umpires.

The quest for accountability in umpires does not necessarily produce better decisions – still less does it lead to uncomplaining acceptance of what they decide. Electronic line-judging may solve problems, but the election of the Wimbledon referee would not necessarily make Mr McEnroe any happier. The prospect of appeals to television replays would not automatically reduce errors in the hairsbreadth verdicts of cricket umpires.

European experience might encourage the Palace to feel secure in the role allotted to it. If the sovereign were impelled, in a narrowly balanced crisis, to make a decision that could be construed as anti-Labour, it would not in most circumstances be serious. Any decision about who should form a government or whether a dissolution should take place must, after all, be subject to early vindication either by the House of Commons or by the electorate. It would not be taken lightly – if only because everyone connected with the sovereign wishes royal impartiality to be accepted as widely as possible throughout the nation. But the fact remains that decisions can be controversial. The sovereign might, at some point, feel bound to refuse a dissolution to a Labour Prime Minister because, say, an Alliance/Conservative government could find a majority in the House of Commons; the sovereign may see it as correct, during a crisis, to summon an Alliance leader before a Labour leader to form a cabinet. And each of these decisions may be seen by Labour politicians, and by the Labour press, as an establishment deal to do them down. Can the sovereign's liability to incur such suspicions be reduced?

Apart from the right to be informed, to encourage and to warn, unchallenged since Bagehot irreverently set it down in 1866, the sovereign's political functions are limited. However, in a hung parliament situation, the sovereign may not be able to avoid two crucial decisions: 'Who should be summoned to form a government?' and 'In what situations should a dissolution be granted or refused?'

Although there is no possibility of providing categorical answers that would apply in all the circumstances in which these questions might arise, agreement may be quite practicable on guidelines that would produce a generally acceptable set of decision rules for the great majority of situations.

To that we shall return. But any decision rules have to be administered by someone. Should the task be transferred, as Mr Benn would like, from the Sovereign to the Speaker? Mr Benn argues that critical decisions should be reserved to elected persons, responsible to someone. The Sovereign does not fit that bill. However, it must be pointed out that in national life, Britain leaves many umpiring decisions to High Court judges who are irremovable. Does Mr Benn want an elected judiciary? The Speaker, too, is virtually irremovable; once chosen each Speaker has, since 1835, been re-elected unchallenged by successive Parliaments and has retired voluntarily at a time of his own choosing.

There are also two practical objections to assigning such a task to the Speaker. One is that the Speaker is in limbo at the very time when he might be most needed. The first act of a Parliament is to elect a Speaker. Usually the outgoing Speaker has been available. But in 1951 and 1959 the ex-Speaker left Parliament and there was a vacuum. In the vital days between an election and the meeting of Parliament, there might be no one with the status to act. Even if the outgoing Speaker were available and had every reason to expect re-election, he might be chary of being too activist while awaiting his reappointment.

A more serious objection lies in the nature of the Speaker's office. As Norman St John-Stevas has pointed out, the Speaker is a functionary of Parliament.:

> ... a great, important and respected one no doubt but not a source of authority in his own right ... Involved as he is in the heat of day-to-day political controversy, his non-involvement in political decision-making is an essential prerequisite to the successful discharge of his functions ...
> If MPs knew that the Speaker had the power to dissolve Parliament or choose the Prime Minister, the authority of the chair and of Parliament itself would be seriously weakened.[6]

Most Speakers would be reluctant to act as arbiter on who should be Prime Minister. It is one thing to make day-to-day decisions on procedural priorities, acting by precedent. It is quite another to be a political fixer in the grand manner. The two roles might well conflict. A Speaker who made a controversial decision about the composition of the cabinet might afterwards have difficulty in being accepted as the neutral referee in the ordinary parliamentary skirmishes between the government and opposition benches.

The fact that the Speaker may not be a suitable substitute

for the monarch does not, by itself, invalidate Mr Benn's suggestion. Obviously another umpire could be found, perhaps an ex-Speaker, perhaps the Lord Chief Justice, or, conceivably, a three-man constitutional commission. It would be hard to reach agreement on any such innovation. However, there is also a middle way. Britain could import from the continent that convenient cushion between the Crown and the politicians that has been so successfully developed in Holland, Belgium and Norway: the *informateur*.

6   Is an informateur practicable?   In the democracies of northern Europe the concept of an honest broker, or *informateur*, has been increasingly used to distance the head of state from the rough and tumble of party bargaining. When the parliamentary situation is indeterminate, it is obvious that an experienced and trusted politician, with a licence to consult confidentially with anyone, has a good chance of discovering the leader and the combination of parties that would be most likely to command a majority in Parliament. If the *informateur* unluckily gets the answer wrong, he and not the sovereign takes the blame.

If Britain were to develop a much more complex party situation and the Palace and the politicians decided that an *informateur* would help with the dilemmas in cabinet-forming, to whom would we turn? In Norway the Speaker has sometimes been used. But in Britain we have no Speaker in between Parliaments and, as we have argued, the Speaker from the last Parliament, awaiting re-election, might be very reluctant to undertake any such task. It might be possible to recruit an ex-Speaker – but such a person is not always available or in good health. Another source of appropriate talent might lie in ex-Prime Ministers – but in our very partisan politics, would Labour MPs accept the neutrality of Mr Macmillan or Mr Heath? Would Conservatives be satisfied about the disinterestedness of Sir Harold Wilson or Mr Callaghan? Jo Grimond, eminent ex-cabinet minister, Lord Carr of Hadley, or Lord George-Brown, would probably be no more acceptable.

One might look for an ex-Lord Chancellor, like Lord Elwyn-Jones or Lord Gardiner. One might turn to a more neutralized ex-politician like Lord Shawcross or Lord Robens – but they, too, evoke memories of a controversial past. One might appoint a veteran judge like Lord Denning or Lord Devlin – but judges are not necessarily the best versed in the nuances of Westminster politics. Other possibilities might be ex-Secretaries of the Cabinet, like Lord Trend or Lord Hunt, or an ex-Secretary from the Palace, like Lord Charteris, or even that ultimate conciliator, Lord Goodman. All these eminent persons would doubtless exercise their good offices with subtlety and honour. But it is not obvious that the appointment of any of them would meet with universal and rapturous acceptance. It is, in fact, hard to see, in the short run, any abandonment of the Palace's traditional role as its own *informateur*. Nor is there any reason to suppose that anyone else would necessarily do the job better than the Palace, with all its anxious preparation for the task. It is only if crises become a habit and the machinery creaks loudly that Britain is likely to turn explicitly to an *informateur* to oil the wheels of government-forming. If the arguments get rough, it may indeed become necessary to distance the sovereign from controversy. Meanwhile, the sovereign's Private Secretary may prove an efficient and acceptable, albeit unpublicized, *informateur*. And, as one shrewd observer noted, 'if he were to be badly wrong-footed, he could protect the sovereign by resigning'.

One argument sometimes advanced for letting things continue as before is that making a change would itself be controversial. There is reason to suppose that the Palace, while prepared to be infinitely cautious and discreet in the use of its residual powers, has no mind to give them up. The monarchy undoubtedly retains enormous popular support and, provided it does not act in a provocative way, politicians would be loth to make it a centre of dispute. Any formal alteration in the mode of selecting Prime Ministers would, in present times, stir up a hornet's nest, a noisy and unprofitable argument about a non-problem.

Moreover, a strong case can be made for the *status quo*. If what is feared is arbitrary or partisan behaviour by the head of state, this is more likely to come from an elected President, or an appointed Governor-General, or even a Speaker chosen by Parliament, than from a hereditary sovereign. The temporary heads of state know that in a few years they will be out of their largely ceremonial offices: the selection and dismissal of Prime Ministers offers them their one chance to make a mark on history, and they can be tempted to arbitrary action. In 1975, Sir John Kerr, the Governor-General of Australia, facing a delicate situation, dismissed the Prime Minister and asked the Leader of the Opposition to take office and to advise an election, providing a 'caretaker' administration until the election was decided: he acted abruptly and in a way that came to be widely seen as counter-productive. It does not seem likely that the Queen would have acted in so controversial a fashion. A Speaker would, indeed, be much more likely than a sovereign to try Sir John Kerr's draconian approach to a constitutional dilemma. The Queen has an overwhelming incentive to act justly and to be seen to act justly: a heavy long-term price would be paid for any arbitrary initiative by the Palace, if a significant segment of the political community came to regard it, rightly or wrongly, as partisan.

The role of the constitutional umpire is limited; moreover, the umpire's decisions are open to immediate repudiation by Parliament or by the electorate. No umpire likes having his decisions reversed, especially if he, and his children after him, are condemned to continue as umpire for the indefinite future. The present system, with its present occupants, probably offers as good a guarantee of cautious, prudent umpiring in government crises as Britain is likely to get.

Moreover, as we shall see, substantial steps could be taken to diminish the both the number and the nature of the dilemmas left for the umpire to resolve.

7 If the Prime Minister resigns, does the Queen ask him for advice on his successor? Does he volunteer it?

As far as we know, advice has seldom been given in recent times. When the outcome of an election has been clear, the soverign has not sought advice from the outgoing Prime Minister. There is no reason to suppose that it was sought in any of the recent transitions between parties – in 1945, 1951, 1964, 1970, 1974 or 1979.[7]

One nice point is that, as soon as a Prime Minister resigns, he forfeits his status as an authoritative giver of advice. If he proposes to advise the sovereign on his successor, he must begin the interview by explaining his intention and then tender any advice he has to offer before he actually gives up the seals of office.

There is certainly no absolute obligation on the sovereign to seek advice or to follow it. In 1908, Lord Esher noted that Lord Knollys, the King's Private Secretary, 'is anxious to discover the views of the Cabinet [about a successor to the dying Campbell-Bannerman]. That is impossible. The King must use his own judgment.'[8]

Ivor Jennings is equally explicit about what must happen when a government is defeated:

> Where there is a leader of the Opposition the [Sovereign] must send for him. [This] rule has as its corollary the rule that, before sending for the Leader of the Opposition, the Monarch should consult no-one. If he takes advice first, it can only be for the purpose of keeping out the Opposition or its recognised leader. To try to keep out the Opposition is to take sides in a party issue. To try to defeat the claims of the recognised leader is to interfere in the internal affairs of the chief Opposition party.[9]

8 Is there any necessary sequence that the Palace should follow in summoning potential Prime Ministers? It might save the sovereign from controversy if it were generally accepted that she must ask the parties in order of size. In Scenario A, set out at the beginning of this chapter, if the leader of the Conservatives with 215 seats resigned, would it be quite automatic that she would call the Labour leader with 210 seats, before calling the leader of Alliance with 200? Many would argue that such would undoubtedly be the proper course. But there are three possible difficulties.

The most trivial lies in the arithmetic of a close-run situation. One or two vacant seats or potential floor-crossers may, in a post-election situation, leave in doubt which party is in fact the second largest.

A second, more serious difficulty lies in the treatment of linked parties. Let us envisage a situation where the Alliance had 210 and Labour 200 seats. It would be open to Labour to say that the Alliance was two parties not one; since Labour had more seats than either the Liberals or the SDP separately, it should take priority. Or, to take an opposite case, if Labour had 210 seats and the Alliance 200, could the Alliance, after reaching a quick agreement with 12 of the supporters of minor parties, claim that its 212 seats now gave it priority?

The third and biggest difficulty lies in the sequel to the summons. Let us consider one particularly difficult scenario – an outcome, after a Conservative government had appealed to the country, such as this:

Conservative	230
Labour	270
Alliance	120
Other	20

The Alliance indicate that they would work under a Conservative government but not under its current Leader.

The Labour party makes plain (as it did in 1974) that it is ready to form a minority government but not to make deals with any other party. The Conservative Prime Minister goes to the Palace and, before resigning, indicates that the Conservative Deputy Leader should be asked to form a government, assured of Alliance support. Should the Queen accept this advice or should she send for the Leader of the largest party, Labour? It is a no-win situation. Whichever course was followed would be regarded as violently objectionable by a large section of the political community. Here two widely accepted principles are irreconcilable:

1 If a party is defeated in an election, the sovereign sends for the Leader of the Opposition in the previous parliament, especially if it is now the largest party.

2 The sovereign sends for the leader most likely to command a majority in the House of Commons.

There are many people, from all points in the political spectrum, who would argue that the Queen should certainly send for the Labour Leader, ask him to form a government and, if he is defeated at the first vote, grant a request for a dissolution. She would be following precedent and she would be referring the decision to the voters. But she would also, at a time when Parliament offered a viable government, be giving to Labour the chance of choosing a polling day and going to the country with all the prestige of a government in office. There is, moreover, a paradox. If the Conservative Leader (by private agreement with the Alliance) stayed in office until Parliament met and confirmed a coalition government in power, then there could be no objection in the event of a Prime Minister resigning if a successor was found from within the ranks of the coalition. Once a government is established, there is no reason for the sovereign to send for the Leader of the Opposition, even if it is the largest party in the House, should the Prime Minister resign or die in office.

But, in the event of the Prime Minister resigning immediately, the snag about the alternative course is that the coalition might not stick together. How far could the Queen accept the assurance that there was a working majority? In 1926 Lord Byng was told by Mr Meighen that he could command a majority in the Canadian House of Commons. Events proved that he did not – to the humiliation of Lord Byng and his office.

However, if the Labour Leader was summoned, it would certainly raise questions about the nature of the commission he was given and his right to a dissolution.

9 What commission does the sovereign give to anyone she summons?   On most occasions when a Prime Minister has been called to the Palace he at once 'kisses hands upon his appointment as Prime Minister and First Secretary of the Treasury'. But delay is possible. On Thursday 17 October 1963, the Queen asked Lord Home to see if he could form a government. He was not appointed Prime Minister until 24 hours later when he had received assurances that almost all the former cabinet would serve under him. Of course, in that case all that was needed was enough time to check on the internal position within the hierarchy of one party. If several parties were involved (and some were under a commitment to consult their wider membership) the delay would have to be much greater. And even then there could be uncertainty about whether the appointee would, in fact, win a vote in the House of Commons. However, without a great change in custom, there would be no question of making the new appointment contingent upon such a vote. Under present practice the new government can face the House of Commons and present a Queen's Speech only as a duly appointed cabinet under a full-fledged Prime

Minister. The Swedish or German requirement, by which the head of government has to secure a parliamentary vote before assuming office, has its conveniences, even though it is a very long way from British precedent.

However, at the time of a conditional appointment or of a formal appointment, it is possible that either the sovereign or the appointee may make conditions. Certainly, helped by *informateurs*, the head of state in continental countries has on occasion specified that it should be or that it should not be a minority government. Here, in 1931, Macdonald was charged with forming a National Government. And in 1910, although admittedly not on taking office, Asquith reached some conditional understandings with the King on the questions of dissolution and the creation of peers.

A potential Prime Minister, not yet endorsed by any vote of the House of Commons, does not have the same rights or freedoms as a properly entrenched holder of the office. It may be necessary for the sovereign to lay down conditions both of time and of substance when asking someone to try to form a government. Would it not be reasonable to set a time limit on the attempt or to ask that any government formed should have the prospect of a parliamentary majority? Unless this is done, any candidate for Prime Minister, called in due sequence on the basis of his party's size, could form a minority government and, on defeat in parliament, ask for an immediate dissolution. Some would say that this would be in order. Parties do not provoke elections unless they think they are going to do well out of them; if the minority Prime Minister appealed to the country and won, that would solve the crisis. If he failed to win, the situation would at least be clarified and future politician chary of following such a course again. This might prove an expensive form of national political education. However, there is perhaps a further safeguard. The public does not like too frequent elections, as is demonstrated by the reluctance of politicians in every country to call them close together.[10]

10 What determines whether there should be coalition government or minority government?   If the price is not too high, governing parties would always prefer to have the assurance of the sustained tenure of office that a solidly-based' coalition will give them. But the price can easily be too high. The dominant party may have to water down its programme too heavily; the smaller party may lose its identity and be blamed for all the sins of its larger partners. The electoral consequences of coalitions may be disastrous for each of the parties involved.

As we have seen, following indeterminate election results, Britain and Canada have gone for minority governments rather than coalitions. The first-past-the-post electoral system has fostered this tendency in two ways. On the one hand, it offers to any party the prospect that the next election will give it unfettered power. Diefenbaker in 1957-8, Trudeau in 1972-4, and Wilson in 1974 won a clear majority at a second election after presiding over a minority government. On the other hand, first-past-the-post voting makes life difficult for coalition partners. Some electoral deal is necessary if they are not to lose seats on split votes; but electoral deals that involve local candidates standing down in favour of another party can have a devastating effect on local organization and morale. The coalition partners face the harsh choice between, destructively from the point of view of winning seats, fighting each other in the constituencies, or, equally destructively from the point of view of preserving party identity and structure, collaborating with each other in the constituencies. If the electoral deal does not lead to fusion, it leads to frustration and feuding. What happened in March 1974 was more or less inevitable; the Liberals had to refuse a coalition with the Conservatives; the Labour party had to go it alone and look to a new election to solve the problem. When, in 1977, the Liberals made a limited deal with Labour, it was on the clear understanding that they would in due course break away and fight the election independently.

Proportional representation would make the situation doubly different. On the one hand, as everyone involvolved would recognize, a new election would not produce a clear result; the acceptance that a stable government with a lasting parliamentary majority could only be secured by an inter-party deal, would put the parties under great pressure to make the deal straightaway. On the other hand, when an election finally came, coalition partners would be able to fight each other in the constituencies without giving away seats on a split vote.

It is thus not by chance that, in countries with proportional representation, minority governments have been exceptional and coalitions the norm.

11 What should happen if there is uncertainty about who should be treated as the effective leader of a party? Elections can bring individual as well as party disasters. Party leaders may be defeated in their own constituencies as Balfour was in 1906, Asquith in 1918 and 1924, and MacDonald in 1918 and 1935. In 1983 or 1984, for example, it is possible to conceive of the Alliance doing well in the election but of Roy Jenkins losing Hillhead. In itself, a Leader's defeat would present no insuperable obstacle to negotiations. As Sir Alec Douglas-Home showed in 1963, a man can be Prime Minister while waiting to get back to the House of Commons. But the authority of a seatless leader would undoubtedly be diminished; and who, remembering Patrick Gordon-Walker's fate in Leyton in 1965, could guarantee that nothing would go wrong with the by-election?

A more serious problem would arise if the election had so diminished the authority or the will of a party Leader that he was unwilling to carry on. In the old days 'magic circles' would have worked swiftly or deputies would have taken over. But now that all parties have developed elaborate election procedures, the difficulties of enthroning a new Leader are considerable. And a Deputy Leader who was a candidate for the succession would be much inhibited in what he did as Acting Leader.

A further problem could arise arise if, during coalition negotiations, a deep rift on tactics developed within a party of a sort that made it plain that the Leader was in a minority among his own MPs. Changing horses in mid-stream presents problems. Even if the outgoing leader were fully co-operative, a smooth and swift handover to an agreed successor would not be easy. If the Leader refused to give way, delays would be considerable.

At the moment, the Conservatives choose their Leader with a three-stage ballot of MPs that, in theory, takes three weeks. In 1975, when it was settled after two stages, it lasted from 23 January to 11 February. Obviously, the Chairman of the 1922 Committee could expedite proceedings by insisting on, say, two days rather than one week between each ballot.

The Labour party now elects its Leader by an elaborate process in which nominees from the Parliamentary Party are submitted to a special delegate conference, with trade unions, constituency parties and the PLP voting separately. Even if, in a crisis, the National Executive Committee were willing to accelerate every part of the operation from the nomination period and delegate consultation to the conference vote, it is hard to see how it could be completed in less than three weeks.

The Liberal party elects its Leader by a vote of all constituency associations, choosing between candidates nominated by the Parliamentary Party. In 1976 the process took from 12 May to 7 July. Doubtless it could be expedited but at the least two or three weeks would be needed.

The Social Democrats elect their Leader by a postal

ballot, with all their members voting on nominees from the Parliamentary Party. In 1982 the process took from late May to 2 July. Again, in a crisis, with co-operation from all sides, a minimum of two weeks would still be needed.

Often, in all parties, it would be plain from the start who the new leader would be. But even the most confidently tipped of winners would be reluctant to act as though the election were a formality. World history is littered with leaders brought down by hubris.

We have to accept that if, in any party at the centre of a cabinet-forming crisis, there is a hiatus in leadership, delay will be inevitable. A party in the throes of a leadership contest is in no position to negotiate. The urgency of the situation will doubtless abbreviate the procedures, because everyone can see that so long as their party lacks a spokesman with full authority, they must be at a disadvantage. However, weeks rather than days may have to elapse before a leadership election is complete.

12 Can the Palace treat with anyone except a party leader?   Let us suppose that in Scenario A, the Conservative Leader with 215 seats was resolutely opposed to doing a deal with the Alliance with 200, but that there were clear indications that the bulk of the party were willing to follow the Deputy Leader into a coalition; would it be proper for the Palace to make contact with the Deputy Leader?

Obviously in such situations most of the business would be done in the political arena, with the principal party figures putting out feelers publicly and privately, holding meetings and caballing. As in August 1931, the Palace might well be presented with something near to a *fait accompli*, with the understandings between the leading actors already concluded. But this cannot be guaranteed. In fact, in August 1931 Lloyd George, the Liberal Leader, was ill and, in the end, dissociated himself from the coalition that his deputy had entered into. On the other hand, the Palace never made contact with anyone in the Labour party other than MacDonald who, though Leader, carried the support of less than 5 per cent of his MPs: he was treated throughout as the sole spokesman for the Labour benches. Arthur Henderson, who certainly represented the bulk of the Labour party, was not consulted.

If parties split or become factionalized, the business of negotiation cannot, even formally, be confined to the elected party Leaders. As in Belgium and Italy, alternative figures within the larger parties may at different times prove to be the most acceptable Prime Ministers. Winston Churchill was Prime Minister for six months in 1940 while Neville Chamberlain continued as party Leader. But that was in an exceptional situation. It would involve a large leap from normal custom for differing figures within the hierarchy of a party to assume the top national office unless they were also taking over the formal leadership of their party. However, if Britain were to move into a world where coalition was the norm rather than the exception, party ties might be much loosened. We should have to think the unthinkable. Quite new conventions, including the acceptance of circulation among top personnel, might be needed.

13 What is the position of the parliamentary parties and of the parties in the country during such a crisis? In past situations, cabinet-forming negotiations have been confined to an elite. In 1915 and 1916, as well as in 1931 and 1940, a few front benchers met together and settled the issue (though in May 1940 by chance the Labour Party Conference was in session and endorsed Mr Attlee's action in joining the coalition). In March 1974 Mr Heath talked to Mr Thorpe who did consult with his thirteen fellow MPs before refusing to collaborate. In March 1977 Mr Steel met with all the Liberal MPs before entering into the Lib-Lab pact; his action was not fully matched by Mr Callaghan, and Mr Steel later regretted that he had not insisted on the pact being explicitly endorsed by the Parliamentary Labour Party.

There is no doubt that nowadays the popular ethos makes it much less likely that party leaders will make deals without endorsement from their parliamentary party – and even their mass followers. In extending the Lib-Lab pact to cover the 1977-8 session, David Steel felt obliged to call a special Assembly of his party at Blackpool in January 1978 to obtain formal support for his decision. The Liberals and the Social Democrats would certainly follow a similar process in the future and it is hard to envisage any Labour leader entering a coalition without seeking prior endorsement from the National Executive of his party.

The need for this wider formal endorsement does not make negotiations easier. Belgian politicians have attributed the recent protraction of their crises in part to the greater intrusion of their followers into the bargaining process. But there can be no doubt of the growing pressures within each of the parties for increasing the accountability by leaders of the rank-and-file. Involvement in a coalition must have far-reaching implications for the identity of any party; it will never happen without heart-searching and some measure of revolt. It would be desirable if, in advance of such a crisis occurring, each party could give some thought to the most acceptable mode of internal consultation.

The details of bargaining and the specific problems of dissolution are dealt with in following chapters. But three more general questions remain to be touched on.

14 Do voting figures matter? Of the two elements in an election result the margin in seats plainly counts for far more than the share of the votes. The February 1974 outcome presented two interesting quantitative challenges. Look at the figures:

TABLE 17
General election 28 February 1974

	Seats	Votes %	
Conservative	207	37·9	635 *seats*
Labour	301	37·1	318 *seats needed*
Liberal	14	19·3	*for majority*
Others	23	5·7	

If the Conservatives had won 301 seats and Labour 297, being therefore four seats ahead instead of four seats behind, the essential logic of the situation would not have been changed. Mr Heath would still have needed both Liberal and Ulster Unionist support to command a majority. But, having most seats, the pressure on him to relinquish office at once would have been greatly reduced. Some senior Conservatives have argued that in such a case they would certainly have stayed on until defeated in Parliament. There is a kind of mysticism about pluralities in seats which politicians find hard to shake off.[11] Whether a party is seen to have won or lost an election is a psychic judgement, a complicated assessment based on the cause of the appeal to the country, the nature of the campaign arguments, and the extent of party gains and losses in seats and votes.

But is there then any sanction in a plurality of votes as distinct from a plurality of seats? In terms of voting percentages the Conservatives 'won' the February 1974 election. 200,000 more people (0.8 per cent) voted for them than for Labour. But, interestingly, they made little play with this 'injustice'. It was the same in 1929 (when

Conservatives got more votes but fewer seats than Labour) and in 1951 (when Labour got more votes but fewer seats than the Conservatives). In 1929 Baldwin explicitly stressed the fact that Labour had got more seats as the reason for his immediate resignation (in contrast to 1923). It is the parliamentary arithmetic that counts, not the psephological fairness of the situation.

Yet voting figures may not be wholly irrelevant. It is important to remember that the gap between the leading parties in 1929, in 1951 and in 1974 was under 1 per cent of the vote. In the future as the scenarios at the beginning of this chapter show, much greater anomalies are likely in a multi-party situation. Consider Scenario A, where Labour has ten more seats than the Alliance but 7 per cent less of the vote: such figures might have some moral force in the bargaining that followed. Consider another, not impossible, scenario; if, under our present first-past-the-post system, a Labour party with 32 per cent joined forces with a Scottish Nationalist party with 2 per cent of the UK vote to produce a majority which denied power to a Conservative party and an Alliance grouping which jointly had drawn 60 per cent of the vote, how fully would the legitimacy of such a government be accepted by the public? In the old days, governments that exercised unfettered authority had, in practice at least, the support of 40 per cent or more of the vote.

15 Is the situation different in mid-Parliament? An election is, as Namier said, a lock on the canal of British history. It is acknowledged as a moment of change. Special rules apply to its aftermath which may not be so appropriate a few months or a few years later. When the British electorate have just voted, it is probably inappropriate to seek the solution to a governmental crisis by yet another appeal to it. But a few months or a few years later the seeking of a new mandate may well be the best answer. Denmark bars a new election for six months and other countries have similar tacit understandings. The rules about a Prime Minister's right to call for a dissolution might well be made to depend on how long the Parliament or the government had lasted. The action of the German Free Democrats in September 1982 in breaking up the SPD/FDP coalition, which they had been elected to support two years earlier, aroused much adverse comment. If hung parliaments become the norm, either through the adoption of proportional representation or the mere chance of multi-party politics, the British Parliament may have to take over from the public as the electoral college, choosing the ministry; the House of Commons will be forced to resume the elective task that Bagehot assigned to it in 1865. After an election it may take a few weeks to sort out the implications and to decide what viable government can be found from within a new Parliament. But if, after some months or years, the whole complexion of the cabinet is suddenly transformed without reference to the electorate, public resentment is bound to follow.

The rules that the sovereign or the politicians should follow would have to be different on day 1 and day 500 of a Parliament's 1800 day life. It is hard to specify the differences, apart from a possible bar on dissolution before, say, six months had passed. But it is clear that the whole spirit of the situation would be transformed, month by month, as the last election receded.

16 How far can any mechanistic rules be laid down?   It is plain, both from common sense and continental experience, that exact prescriptions for the conduct of crises cannot be provided. The Swedish Constitution charges the Speaker with nominating a Prime Minister and sets a short time limit before a parliamentary vote. The

German Basic Law lays down a clear procedure for the election of the Chancellor by the Bundestag. But nearly everywhere else the affair is almost wholly regulated by custom: nowhere, for example, does that ubiquitous aid, the *informateur*, have constitutional status. Yet in most countries, there has developed a clearly understood pattern of behaviour, a regular sequence of consultations, an agreed rhythm in extracting a new government from an indeterminate parliamentary situation. Politicians will, of course, act individually and arrive at private deals, but the central process by which the decisions are officially made on who should form a government, and on how it should move to parliamentary endorsement, have become ritualized. If Britain makes a habit of having governmental crises, it will, inevitably, make a habit of the procedures by which they are solved. Like the rest of the constitution these may stay very largely unwritten in any formal or mandatory way, but (and this is the central theme of this book) they need not stay unchronicled or uncriticized. It is even possible that, in a time of political tranquillity, a Royal Commission or an inter-party conference might thrash out some of the problems and offer some model rules to guide the Palace and the politicians when the crisis actually comes.

Obviously such rules will and need not cover all contingencies. No one could lay down in detail how every participant should act. New and unforeseeable situations will arise and new precedents will be created. But, despite the fact that many things cannot be prescribed in advance, there is still much to be gained from a thorough consideration of the problems. A theatrical director does not abandon all preparations because, with improvisations, 'it will be all right on the night'. In politics improvisation carried too far becomes high-handedness. It leaves a trail of grievance which may beget arbitrariness by the other side when its turn comes. It can even be the stuff of revolution.

There is one Commonwealth case which illustrates

beautifully not only the problem of defining when the head of state can intervene decisively, but also the issue of whether the powers and duties of the head of state can be laid down precisely in debate or constitution. In 1962, the Governor of Western Nigeria, the Oni of Ife, on receiving a letter signed by 66 members (a majority of the House) saying that they no longer had confidence in the Premier, dismissed him. The Nigerian Supreme Court held that he had acted improperly because the letter was an informal communication and that, under the very detailed Nigerian Constitutions, he could intervene only on the basis of an explicit vote in Parliament. The Nigerian Chief Justice said:

> To my mind the conclusion is inescapable that the framers of the Constitution wanted the House to be responsible at every level for the ultimate fate of the Government and the Premier. The horizon must be higher than leaving it to one man. The Governor might eventually be the instrument used to effect this, but his position as final arbiter must be dictated by events in the House or events emanating from the House and not by a letter, however well meaning, signed by a body of members of the House. Law and convention cannot be replaced by party political moves outside the House.
> I belive that the Constitution contemplated proceedings in the House as being the touchstone of whether the Premier (and his Government) commands the support of a majority of the members or no longer commands such support.
> ... It will be an unduly narrow and restrictive interpretation of the powers of the House, and a correspondingly unduly wide interpretation of the powers of the Governor, if, in the circumstances, section 33 (10) is interpreted in any other way except in a way which makes it clear that the evidence emanates from proceedings in the House.[12]

However the issue was appealed to the Privy Council in London which reversed the decision. Lord Radcliffe reflected on United Kingdom usage:

> Another argument has been advanced to the effect that the

Nigerian Constitutions are modelled on the current constitutional doctrines of the United Kingdom, and, since the
British Sovereign would not be regarded as acting with
constitutional propriety in dismissing a Prime Minister from
office without the foundation of an adverse vote on a major
issue in the House of Commons, so the Governor in Western
Nigeria must similarly be treated as precluded from exercis-
ing his power of removal in the absence of a vote of the same
kind. This approach to the matter appears to their Lordships
to have had some influence upon the view taken by the
majority of the Federal Supreme Court in this case, and, since
it seems capable of conveying an implication that could be
misleading in other situations apart from the present one,
their Lordships wish to make two observations upon it.

The first is that British constitutional history does not offer
any but a general negative guide as to the circumstances in
which a Sovereign can dismiss a Prime Minister. Since the
principles which are accepted today began to take shape with
the passing of the Reform Bill of 1832 no British Sovereign
has in fact dismissed or removed a Prime Minister, even
allowing for the ambiguous exchanges which took place
between William IV and Lord Melbourne in 1834. Discussion of constitutional doctrine bearing upon a Prime
Minister's loss of support in the House of Commons
concentrates therefore upon a Prime Minister's duty to ask
for liberty to resign or for a dissolution, rather than upon the
Sovereign's right of removal, an exercise of which is not
treated as being within the scope of practical politics. In this
state of affairs it is vain to look to British precedent for
guidance upon the circumstances in which or the eventual
material upon which a Prime Minister can be dismissed,
where dismissal is an actual possibility: and the right of
removal which is explicitly recognized in the Nigerian
Constitutions must be interpreted according to the wording
of its own limitations and not to limitations which that
wording does not import.

The second observation is perhaps only another way of
making the same point. It is true that the Western Nigerian
Constitution, allowance made for the federal structure, does

embody much of the constitutional practice and principle of the United Kingdom. That appears from a study of its terms. There are identifiable differences of scheme to be found in certain sections, but no one, it seems, questions the general similarity or the origin of many of its provisions. But, accepting that, it must be remembered that, as Lord Bryce once said, the British Constitution 'works by a body of understandings which no writer can formulate'; whereas the Constitution of Western Nigeria is now contained in a written instrument in which it has been sought to formulate with precision the powers and duties of the various agencies that it holds in balance. That instrument now stands in its own right; and, while it may well be useful on occasions to draw on British practice or doctrine in interpreting a doubtful phrase whose origin can be traced or to study decisions on the Constitutions of Australia or the United States where federal issues are involved, it is in the end the wording of the Constitution itself that is to be interpreted and applied, and this wording can never be overridden by the extraneous principles of other Constitutions which are not explicitly incorporated in the formulae that have been chosen as the frame of this Constitution.[13]

Lord Radcliffe's judgement makes many interesting points. The most striking is that, despite the serious attempt by the authors of the Nigerian Constitutions to clarify how a head of state should behave, in the end the Privy Council decided that the Governor was right to act on the basis of an informal unofficial communication. A comprehensive set of rules failed to produce an unambiguous answer. But Lord Radcliffe also makes plain how limited may be the guidance offered by precedent.

It is certainly not the contention of this book that an explicit set of decision rules about the formation and dismissal of governments could or should be laid down. It is hard to see any benefit to the country if the procedures followed during a crisis could become matters of litigation. But there are some key points which obviously could provoke disputes and recrimination. If these can be identified in advance and publicly discussed, it may be possible to achieve some consensus about the least controversial way of reaching solutions. The next two chapters focus on some of these central problems.

CHAPTER SIX

The Nature of the Bargain

PARTIES TO A COALITION require an elaborate set of understandings with each other if they are to make a governing formula work. There will almost certainly be some kind of formally written treaty laying down the main principles of their co-operation; but they will also have a wide range of explicit, or implicit, expectations about how each should behave. Some of these will be based on the ordinary conventions of British politics, but some will have their origins in personal conversations, or even in nods and winks, between the leading actors.

A coalition may emerge from a hectic few days of bargaining (as it did in 1931) but in most cases there will be roots going much further back to informal chats or deliberate discussions between politicians, to expectations built up by the media, and to party programmes and campaign promises. In the end, however, it will be a deal worked out between politicians. Politicians are practitioners in the art of the possible, but they are also individuals with differing public and private goals. Some will have gone into parliament to further specific policies. Some will just want to see their party succeed. Some are there to get office for themselves. Most share all three objectives – but in widely varying degrees.

The negotiations will be shaped by each side's assessment of how much the other side wants office, and by the value it puts on its favourite policies, as well as by its estimate of the electoral consequences of participation in, or exclusion from, the government. The final settlement will be based on a more or less realistic assessment of mutual strength. A distinction should be made between a 'no majority' situation, where no party is anywhere near to an overall lead, and a 'near majority' situation, where one party is so close to the break-even point (326 in a House of 650) that it is clear that no other party could provide a viable government (one thing that is certain is that in no circumstances could all the minority party MPs be corralled into the one government camp).

A coalition made from two groupings, one with 170 MPs and one with 160 MPs will be very different from a coalition based upon groupings of 300 and 30. But obviously numbers are not the sole element: in each of these examples the smaller party is indispensable for the securing of a parliamentary majority. How hard it can bargain will depend on what other alliances are open to either party, and on the electoral prospects of each. Unless the duration of parliaments becomes fixed, the threat of dissolution will hang over every negotiation; parties will always wonder whether the electorate will reward or punish them for intransigence and whether the outcome of a fresh election would leave them in a better or worse bargaining position – or in no bargaining position at all.

Any bargaining will be conditioned by the extent of mutual trust, principally at the elite level, but also in the mass parties. Most elected politicians will, in the last resort, make a deal with almost anyone; ordinary party workers, being farther from power, are more likely to be absolutist and uncompromising. But even at the top there are many dislikes and old scores between politicians to get in the way of sensible agreements (although there are some surprising cross-party friendships that may help to oil creaking negotiations). It is not practicable here, or anywhere perhaps, to assess just how far personal liking or personal animus can determine inter-party relations. But it is worth stressing that, as in international diplomacy, it can help to have several lines of communication open, so that individual hostilities can be by-passed and so that alternative ideas can be explored at different levels and be accepted, modified, or rejected without openly giving victories or snubs to the principal actors. At various points in the 1970s one or two such lines were opened up through junior figures (only, in some cases, to be closed down by their more nervous seniors). In a situation where no clear majority seems likely, some contacts are bound to develop, although they must, of necessity, be very discreet. Any such activity could be wholly counter-productive if it became widely known during a campaign. The electorate, and even more the party faithful, would see such moves as defeatist. Denials would have to be issued that could tie the hands of negotiators when, after the election, the real bargaining began.

Of course, in the gossipy, personalized world of politics there will always be amateur *informateurs*, volunteer intermediaries drawn from people partially in the know, sometimes helpful, sometimes a great nuisance. Their activities and the hints they drop will inevitably add to the confused media speculation about what is going on.

As was pointed out in Chapter 4 and Chapter 5, any negotiation will be coloured by the party leaders' uncertainty about their followers. In playing out their hands, each will use as cards 'I'm not sure if I could sell that to my own people', or 'the constituencies would insist absolutely on that', or 'I'd have to put that to the parliamentary party'. The Liberals would want any future deals to be explicitly endorsed by all the MPs of the parties involved. Any Labour leader would face great trouble if he agreed to something against the flat disapproval of the National Executive Committee. Even a Conservative leader, with ancestral memories of 1921-2, would want to feel assured that the National Union and the constituencies would not be too upset.

However, although the show of respect for party democracy would certainly need to be more ostentatious than a generation ago, British parties are still accustomed to strong leadership. Coalition deals have to be prepared within a small elite. It is the job of party leaders to know how far they can take their followers – but they can take them a long way. An assurance that a deal is in the best interests of the party will usually succeed. The danger is less from a revolt from the bottom than from a coup among colleagues. Parties when they split, split from the top.

It is when a significant group of front benchers is ready to break away, probably in the light of rank and file misgivings about an agreement, that a deal is likely to collapse. The problem of a party leader is to keep his immediate colleagues happy; since, in a coalition, jobs have to be shared between two or more parties, the colleagues are bound to be anxious about their own prospects and they may translate potential personal disappointments into party arguments. Coalitions are unlikely to be achieved without recriminations. The art of successful leadership will be to confine the recriminations to the issues or to the people that matter least.

A coalition has to agree on its policy and its personnel. Policy takes most time. The prospective partners will know that their first public action will be the presentation to Parliament of a Queen's Speech, a legislative and administrative policy for the next twelve months. And if they hope to last through a Parliament, they will also be thinking about a second, and even a third and fourth, Queen's Speech.

They have to decide what are the core issues. When they disagree on a problem they have either to compromise or to exclude it. The coalitions formed in 1915, 1931 and 1940 could each be formed very swiftly because they had few declared goals. It was not difficult to agree on winning the war, or even on the 1931 seven-point programme to meet the economic crisis. But such agreements succeeded by a process of exclusion, by begging all the detailed questions, those problems that always take so long in Dutch and Belgian cabinet-forming.

Some fringe issues can of course be side-stepped (even though governments are still liable to fall in arguments over trivia. Core issues of economic or defence policy cannot be fudged beyond a certain point, although sometimes they can be postponed to a later review, referred to a committee, or left to a free vote in Parliament.

Any deals, however, that are meant to last must have built into them some formula for reconciling major differences on key questions. A limited demonstration of the problem was available in 1982 when the Liberals and Social Democrats could be observed attempting to merge into a common programme their differing views on nuclear weapons, on incomes policy and on devolution.

After an election in which two parties have fought separately on conflicting manifestos it may be harder to get them to abandon the positions they have been vigorously propounding to the voters. Yet the Queen's Speech has to be prepared in a matter of days. Unless the country faces so acute a crisis that a doctor's mandate is acceptable ('My government will prepare any measures that seem necessary to meet the nation's predicament'), the coalition has to spell out its approach to such difficult questions as public sector pay and state intervention in industrial relations, policies for the nationalized industries and for the social services, attitudes to taxation and to public expenditure, to the European Community and to NATO, as well as a stance on institutional issues like the second chamber, devolution and electoral reform. All these matters will doubtless have been the subject of extended study by each party. In a crisis situation each may, in a few hours, have to consent to abandon or to compromise positions taken up over several years.

As the agreement is about people as much as about

programmes, there is likely to be some trade-off between patronage and policies. For some, at least, who gets what job will matter much more than what they do with it. But, significantly, in most continental countries the policy deal is completed before the allocation of portfolios.

In nations accustomed to coalitions, offices are usually distributed between the parties in fairly close proportion to parliamentary representation. Where this arithmetic is deviated from, it is to give to a key small party rather more than its fair share of portfolios. In the 1931 National Government, the National Labour group was grossly overrepresented. In 1940 the Liberals were generously treated. Sometimes, as in Israel and Fourth Republic France, new offices are created *ad hoc* to ease the problem of achieving an acceptable balance.

One special problem that would arise in Britain flows from the size of the ministerial team. In 1979 there were 107 paid government posts – 86 in the Commons and 21 in the Lords. There were fourteen major departments that had between four and seven ministers apiece. Would there be an attempt at proportional representation within each department? Or would complete departments be allocated to parties? If there were, as in past British coalitions, a mix of parties within most departments, would the natural power that goes to the Secretary of State have to be in some way balanced by extra strength for the other side among the junior ministers?

Would some parties in a coalition lay claim to particular ministries? In Australia the Departments of Trade and of Agriculture have normally been reserved for the National Country Party. In Italy the Christian Democrats have vitually monopolized the Interior and Education Departments. In Israel from 1947-77 Mapai/Labour kept exclusive hold on Defence and Foreign Affairs. In Denmark, whenever the Social Democrats have been in office, they have insisted on the Social Affairs and the Labour portfolios. It is less obvious what claims would apply in Britain, and with large ministerial teams offering the possibility of a coalition within each department, the problem may be small.[1]

But patronage extends beyond the allocation of ministerial offices. In many countries the distribution of patronage is the main business of politics. In Britain that element has become smaller since Sir Robert Walpole's day. But very many public appointments are in the gift of the Prime Minister or individual ministers. These appointments have never been made on a narrow party basis but each party has tended to look after its own. Coalition partners are bound to eye each other critically to check that they are not being done down. Implicitly or explicitly there will be constant trade-offs, with the failure to win one coveted job being compensated by preferred treatment over another. With some sense of fair play and competent work by the whips, these matters may be regulated fairly smoothly; but, if there are disputes, they are far more likely to break into the open than when only one party is concerned with government. It may well be that, at the outset of a coalition, some clear agreement over the principles and the procedure of patronage will be needed.

British government has come to turn around the person of the Prime Minister. Is his role negotiable? The Prime Minister's right to appoint, transfer and dismiss ministers is unchallenged. So, too, is the Prime Minister's right to recommend a dissolution. And if the Prime Minister resigns, all other offices are up for disposal. When there has been one-party majority government, as well as during wartime coalitions, this system has worked well enough; we have become completely habituated to Prime Ministerial dominance. But in a coalition between two equally-balanced parties, it would be quite unacceptable to allow a Premier to have the degree of primacy assumed by a Wilson or a Thatcher. The Leader of the second party would need assurances of consultation, probably a veto, over almost all the major powers that Prime Ministers have hitherto exercised unilaterally. Conservatives in 1919-22 greatly resented Lloyd George's high-handed use of his office. Some share-out of authority would be needed – but it would present problems since, formally and informally, the Prime Minister and 10 Downing Street have become the hub of the governmental machine. The Prime Minister's weekly audience with the Queen, the Prime Minister's control over the security services, the Prime Minister's authority over top civil service appointments and the Prime Minister's chairmanship of the cabinet are all matters which a Deputy Prime Minister of another party might resent. And one particular function, the Prime Minister's power to propose and indeed to impose the membership of cabinet committees (where so much of the business of government is done) would have to be placed in commission in any balanced coalition. The Cabinet Office and the Central Policy Review Staff nominally work for the cabinet as a whole but, *de facto* they have often been answerable almost solely to the Prime Minister: they, too, would have to be put in wider hands.

But if the Prime Minister's role is what he makes it to be, so too, in a coalition situation, would be the Deputy Prime Minister's. Even with single party governments the authority of the Prime Minister fluctuates enormously with personality and with circumstance. MacDonald, as a rump Prime Minister in 1931-35, got on well enough with Baldwin at the head of the dominant Conservative party. Attlee secured his own way to a remarkable degree with Churchill in 1940-5. But in a future delicately balanced coalition, the junior partner or partners would certainly want to demand some prior assurances from the Prime Minister.

Who would nominate the persons to hold office? In many countries posts are allocated to parties and party leaders or committees decide who shall fill them. In Australia, the National Country Party ministers have plainly been chosen by the Leader of the National Country Party (who is Deputy

Prime Minister) and not by the Liberal Prime Minister. In Britain, Prime Ministers have usually consulted their Secretaries of State over departmental appointments; but on occasion they have imposed on ministers deputies who were deliberately differentiated, selected either as watchdogs for the Premier or in order to reassure the party or the public outside; that, however, has hardly been a formula for efficient administration. A Prime Minister and a Deputy Prime Minister from different parties could face delicate problems in reconciling their own unavoidable considerations of party management with what is required to produce effective departmental teams.

Any government has to envisage the need for reshuffles. Ministers die, or resign, or prove themselves no good, or get involved in confrontations or political disasters which make a change desirable. Even with single party administrations the formation of a cabinet is a balancing act. With coalitions the problem may be far more difficult. When a leading figure is removed from the cabinet equation, it may not be practicable to find a replacement of similar weight from the same party. When a key office falls vacant, it may seem that, either to make a change or to make no change in the party holding it, will upset the delicate assumptions on which the government was originally formed. It would scarcely be possible for the initial pact to include a blueprint defining who would go where in every hypothetical vacancy and reshuffle. But it would be desirable to have clear understandings on whether specific offices were, or (preferably) were not, to be regarded as the property of one party or the other, as well as on the procedures for inter-party consultations to be followed in any reshuffle.

Negotiations to establish a coalition government will never be easy and there is much to be said for keeping the agenda to a minimum. Many of the problems will be dealt with readily enough by common sense and *ad hoc* compromise. In due course precedents will be established for the handling of many of the problems that cannot be foreseen but that will recur. But it would be helpful if provisional ground-rules could be established to remove from contention some of the problems that might arise in the government-forming negotiations which, if not foreseen at that stage, might bedevil the day-to-day working of the coalition.

Some problems may seem trivial. For example, what would be the conventions about seating in the House of Commons? Would the coalition parties merge indiscriminately behind the front bench? Or would they congregate separately so that the reporters and the Opposition could note more exactly who cheered whom? Prudence would dictate a merger, but vigilance might be needed to deter an unofficial segregation.

More substantially, how would the whipping be managed? Would the coalition whips share a government whips' office or would they disperse in different rooms and negotiate together on each successive issue? Would there be a government Chief Whip or would there be joint Chief Whips? In a coalition situation a central tactic of any opposition will be to drive a wedge between the partners. Skilled handling by the whips will be needed to preserve a reasonable façade of unity.

One element in the deal which, especially at the beginning of a Parliament, may be difficult to plan is the approach to the next election. If all went well with the coalition, would the partners make a joint appeal to the country on a common manifesto? Unless the coalition was breaking up they would have to defend what they had jointly done and what they jointly planned to do. But joint manifestos are a long step along the road to party fusion and may be quite unacceptable to the constituency activists. The ordinary elector may not be interested in the fine points of political ideology which give a party its identity, but to many loyalists these are the very *raison d'être* of their activity.

Obviously, in all this the nature of the electoral system can be decisive. Under most forms of proportional representation coalition partners can exist independently and fight each other at general elections without paying any serious penalty. But under the first-past-the-post system it is disastrous to have two defenders of a coalition splitting the vote. Indeed this problem may threaten a coalition from the very outset. What happens in a by-election? Do the coalition partners in their initial deal include an agreement to give a free run to the incumbent party if a vacancy occurs? If an opposition seat falls vacant, do they leave the contest to whichever of the coalition partners came highest at the general election? These questions may not be difficult to solve but, unless there is advance agreement, they are the stuff of political disputes.

Any agreement between the coalition partners is bound to be a matter of great public interest. In Holland the agreements are normally kept secret; in Israel it is mandatory that they should be made public. In Britain it would be almost inevitable that the deal will be part open, part covert. A statement will be demanded by the media and the broad terms of any agreement will have to be set out more or less publicly if they are to be ratified by the parliamentary parties, national executives, or party conferences. But there will almost certainly be supplementary understandings between the principal actors, agreements about the distribution of patronage and the procedures of consultation which it would be impolitic to advertise.

Coalition governments may endure well beyond expectation, but they do not last for ever. Politicians dislike peering too far into the future, but they cannot enter a coalition without giving some thought to how long it may endure and how it may terminate. Coalitions end, either because circumstances change or because there is disagreement (or even welshing) over the terms of the bargain. Circumstances may change because the death or resignation of some senior minister disturbs the balance of the coalition; they are more likely to change because an issue arises that was either unforeseen, or deliberately unprovided for, in the original bargain. The bargain may break down because it is too ambiguous or because it is not sufficiently comprehensive.

If coalition partners disagree sharply on how to handle an international or an industrial or economic crisis, the government is likely to fall, unless it is apparent to both sides that the electoral consequences of a break-up would be disastrous for their party fortunes. If it is apparent that the electoral system assures the continued parliamentary strength of each partner, the temptation will be for one side to precipitate a crisis, if they think the new deal after the reshuffle may well give them a better hand. But central to all coalition politics is the question of whether the coalition can end without simultaneously ending the Parliament. The constitutional rules and the political understandings about dissolution will determine the behaviour of the co-operating or contending parties. It is to this which we now turn.

CHAPTER SEVEN

The Problem of Dissolution

———————◦◦———————

UNDER A FIRST-PAST-THE-POST ELECTION SYSTEM the dissolution of Parliament always offers an escape route from crisis. It means that the problem is referred to the electors and there is a good chance that their votes will produce a decisive answer, at least in terms of parliamentary seats. Even under a proportional system, a new election may change and clarify the situation by shuffling the parliamentary pack and giving a new indication of popular feeling, even though with proportional representation, it is unlikely that there will be a clear majority for one party, or even a great variation from previous parliamentary strengths.

But what determines when a dissolution should occur? In Britain, since the eighteenth century, the sovereign has always granted a dissolution when the Prime Minister has asked for one. Moreover, in this century at least, it has become accepted that the request for a dissolution is a matter for the Prime Minister alone. Although, as with Mr Wilson in 1970, he may go through the form of discussing the matter in cabinet, he has often acted with minimal consultation. Mr Attlee, for example, gave no advance warning even to the Deputy Prime Minister, Herbert Morrison, of his ending of the 1950-1 Parliament. Mr Baldwin acted by himself in 1923 and, similarly but much less spectacularly, in 1935. The negative as well as the positive decisions on election timing have been the Prime Ministers's own. Sir Alec Douglas-Home did not leave the putting-off of the 1964 election from spring to autumn to the cabinet; still less did Mr Callaghan involve others in his perhaps fateful decision not to go to the country in October 1978.

There is a large body of literature on the power of dissolution. The three most authoritative texts – by Evatt, Forsey, and Markesinis – offer fascinating reading, although many of the points they make are, by now, obsolete.[1] They discuss what the head of state can do within the Westminster model. But, time and again, they conclude that any decisive exercise of a power to enforce or to refuse a dissolution, however constitutional and however well advised, would be controversial and therefore counter-productive to the position which the head of state holds as a unifying symbol, above the party battle.

The literature is full of strong assertions that the sovereign has the right, and, in certain circumstances, the duty to use the royal prerogative unilaterally. A.V.Dicey, for example, defined the royal prerogative as 'the residue of discretionary or arbitrary authority which at any given time is legally left in the hands of the Crown' and argued that the Crown had:

> The right to dismiss a Ministry who command a parliamentry majority and to dissolve the Parliament by which the Ministry are supported ... A dissolution is allowable whenever the wishes of the legislature are, or may be presumed to be, different from the wishes of the nation.[2]

But few would go along with Dicey. His contemporary, that equally conservative constitutionalist, Sir William Anson, certainly maintained that the Prime Minister's advice for dissolution should, as a rule, be accepted. 'It would seem therefore,' he argued, 'that a dissolution is now invariably granted on the request of the minister and involves no rebuff to the sovereign if the minister is defeated at the polls.'[3] Anson approved of Lord Aberdeen saying, 'he had never entertained the slightest doubt that if the minister advised the Queen to dissolve she would, as a matter of course, do so.'[4] However Anson would have joined later writers such as Professor de Smith who, in 1969, was arguing that the sovereign can refuse a request for dissolution if there are 'substantial grounds for believing that a stable government can be formed without an election.'[5] Bonar Law, in a partisan submission to the Palace in 1912, put the reverse of the same coin arguing that:

> The King not only had the constitutional right but that it was his duty before acting on the advice of his Ministers to ascertain whether it was not possible to appoint other Ministers who would advise him differently and allow the question to be decided by the country at a general election.[6]

Although in 1893 Queen Victoria still contemplated unilateral insistence on dissolution, and Bonar Law was advocating it as late as 1913, no one now seriously envisages a situation in which the sovereign would step in positively and dissolve Parliament, except upon the advice of an incumbent Prime Minister. But the opposite to that, the refusal of dissolution, remains a live issue. In 1916 George V made plain, 'that he would refuse, if asked, to accord ... a dissolution', because of the wartime situation. But the King had just been advised by Lord Haldane that once a man had kissed hands as Prime Minister the only alternative to accepting his advice was to dismiss him, which was a dangerous step.[7]

Much of the writing about the royal power to insist on or to refuse dissolutions comes from an older tradition, a tradition which suggests that the sovereign (or, in some cases, the House of Lords) is custodian of a superior wisdom about the state of public opinion. But for the sovereign to assert that ministerial interpretation of public opinion is wrong entails, necessarily, entering the political arena. As Lord Byng found in Canada in 1926, or Sir John Kerr in Australia in 1975, it does not enhance the authority of the office of head of state if the holder feels forced, however unavoidably, into actions which many voters regard, however misguidedly, as partisan.

To refuse a Prime Minister's request for dissolution is, *de facto*, to dismiss him. And, as Asquith pointed out in 1913, if the sovereign does that, 'it is no exaggeration to say that the Crown would become the football of contending factions. That's a constitutional catastrophe which it is the duty of every wise statesman to do his utmost in his power to avert.' Or more bluntly, as Markesinis points out, the King can do no wrong so long as he, 'reigns and does not rule', or, in Bagehot's words, 'if he follows a well considered inaction.'[8]

Are there circumstances in which the Prime Minister's request for a dissolution should be refused? And are the currently accepted conventions appropriate to the possible future situations being considered in this book?

The right to grant or refuse a dissolution is one of the few substantial royal powers that has not atrophied beyond all constitutional dispute. It may not have been used in practice for 200 years. At least 50 dissolutions have been unconditionally granted on advice from a Prime Minister since the sovereign last refused one or unilaterally ordered one. But hypothetical dilemmas have kept the issue alive to the point when the King's Private Secretary could feel forced, as recently as 1950, to send a pseudonymous letter to *The Times* insisting upon the survival of royal discretion over the issue; on 14 May 1950, when Labour was governing with a narrow majority, Sir Alan Lascelles, writing over the signature 'Senex', argued that it would be right to refuse a request for dissolution if it was apparent that an alternative government could command a majority in the Commons. Few today would support his view when applied to a Prime Minister who had been in office for some months and was then defeated. Indeed Mr Wilson seemed to hint in his High Wycombe speech of 14 March 1974 that he had been given an assurance that he could have a dissolution if defeated in the House of Commons, even if the Conservatives in alliance with the Liberals and Ulster Unionists could offer an alternative government. No such assurance had in fact been given but it does seem likely that, if the Queen's Speech had not been endorsed by the House of Commons on 17 March, a dissolution would have been granted.

Real problems do arise at the moment of government-formation. No one suggests that a Prime Minister defeated at an election could expect the sovereign to grant a new dissolution and an immediate rerun of an election. Asquith put the case in December 1923:

> Dissolution of Parliament is in this country one of the prerogatives of the Crown. It is not a mere feudal survival, but it is a part, and I think a useful part, of our constitutional system.... It does not mean that the Crown should act arbitrarily and without the advice of responsible Ministers, but it does mean that the Crown is not bound to take the advice of a particular Minister to put its subjects to the tumult and turmoil of a series of General Elections so long as it can find other Ministers who are prepared to give contrary advice. The notion that a Ministry which cannot command a majority in the House of Commons ... a Ministry in a minority of 31 per cent ... in these circumstances is invested with the right to demand a dissolution is as subversive of constitutional usage, as it would, in my opinion, be pernicious to the general and paramount interest of the Nation at large.[9]

Viscount Simon made the same point in different terms in April 1950 in a letter to *The Times*:

> This 'difficult and intricate question' [of dissolution] cannot be dogmatically answered without considering the circumstances in which it arises ... Is it really suggested that, however recent the last General Election may be and whatever its result, the Prime Minister has the absolute right to require the Crown to put its subjects to the 'tumult and turmoil' of another General Election within a few weeks of the

last? And, if the result of the second election does not suit him, can he claim a third? On the contrary I conceive that the Sovereign has the duty, in the case of a freshly elected Parliament at any rate, of considering whether government could be carried on under another head, and that if he thinks that it can, he is acting constitutionally....

Supposing that, as the result of a General Election, a Prime Minister finds himself left with the support of only a minority in the new House of Commons. He is under no obligation to resign immediately, and his Government may decide to meet the House when it assembles. An amendment to the Address is then carried against them, as happened in 1892. When this happens, can the defeated Prime Minister go to the Sovereign and demand another general election and is the Sovereign bound to grant this request? Of course not. But why not? Because there is an alternative government available without sending the electorate again to the polls.[10]

However, the problem might be seen as different if someone at the head of a new government that had never received any endorsement from the House of Commons were defeated at the first test. Would he have any automatic right to a dissolution? If so, the mere invitation to try to form a government automatically involves jurisdiction over whether and when there should be an election.

The Commonwealth offers several key examples of Prime Ministers being overridden on the question of dissolution. The Western Nigerian case of 1962 was cited at the end of Chapter 5. The first ten years of the Australian Commonwealth saw three refusals of dissolution by the Governor-General on the ground that alternative governments were available in the Federal Parliament. But the most frequently quoted precedents come from 1926, 1932, 1939 and 1975.

In 1926 Viscount Byng, the Governor-General of Canada, refused the Liberal Mackenzie King's request for a dissolution under the mistaken impression that the Conservative Leader, Mr Meighen, could command a parliamentary majority. Mr Meighen had misinformed him about the likely behaviour of the third party, the Progressives. When Mr Meighen's government was immediately defeated in the House of Commons by one vote, there followed an election in which Lord Byng's action became the focus of argument: Mackenzie King won and it became generally apparent that Lord Byng had misjudged the situation. He would have done much better to have dissolved the first time on Mr King's advice, and not to have had the humiliation of dissolving a few days later on Mr Meighen's advice, only to see Mr Meighen defeated. What happened made it unlikely that any subsequent Governor-General would ever refuse a dissolution.

In September 1939 in South Africa the Prime Minister, General Hertzog, found himself in a minority in his cabinet in wanting South Africa to stay neutral in the war. He sought support from Parliament but General Smuts, his Minister of Justice carried an amendment by 80 to 67 supporting a declaration of war. General Hertzog then sought a dissolution. The Governor-General, Sir Patrick Duncan, refused, knowing that a majority of the House and of the cabinet were opposed. General Hertzog resigned. General Smuts took over and stayed securely in office for four years before calling an election.

In New South Wales in 1932, the Governor, Sir Philip Game, dismissed the State Premier, Jack Lang, for insisting on defying a federal law. The Leader of the Opposition took office, accepted responsibility for the Governor's action, asked for a dissolution, and won the ensuing election. In the long subsequent controversy about Sir Philip Game's action, the key point was that the courts could perhaps have offered a remedy against the Premier's 'illegal' actions. Memories of this episode had a powerful influence 43 years later, upon one young observer, John Kerr.

On 11 November 1975, Sir John Kerr, who had been appointed Governor-General of Australia a year earlier on the advice of the Labor Prime Minister, Gough Whitlam, brought about the most spectacular of Commonwealth constitutional crises. Believing that a deadlock between the House and the Senate over supply could be resolved only by a general election, he dismissed Mr Whitlam when he refused to advise one; he then called Malcolm Fraser, the Leader of the Opposition, to be a 'caretaker' Prime Minister on the understanding that he would immediately recommend a dissolution. Mr Fraser won the ensuing election and so, in a sense, Sir John Kerr's action received popular vindication. Yet the whole Labor party and quite a lot of other people (including Sir William McMahon and Sir John Gorton, former Liberal Prime Ministers) believed that the Governor-General had acted wrongly and in a fashion that would warn any successor against so strong an exercise of the head of state's reserve powers. Many aspects of this fascinating case are quite outside our scope here, but it does offer the only recent example of a head of state in a major democracy acting during a crisis in a way that half the nation could regard as arbitrary and partisan.[11]

It is significant that only two written European constitutions give the head of state the power to dissolve Parliament unilaterally. In France this is part of the Gaullist presidential primacy. In West Germany, in the extreme case when the Bundestag fails to elect a Chancellor by a majority vote, the President can choose between accepting a minority Chancellor and calling a new election. But the West German President does also have the power to refuse to accept the advice to dissolve, even when it comes from a majority Chancellor.

Italy allows the President to dissolve, 'after having heard the advice of the Presidents of the two Houses'. Ireland, while allowing the President to dissolve only on the concurring advice of the Prime Minister, gives him power to refuse to do so, 'if the Prime Minister does not command the confidence of the House'. It is notable, however, that no

European king or president since the war seems to have got himself or his office into serious trouble over the exercise – or non-exercise – of the power of dissolution.

Britain, of course, has no constitution and many commmentators rely on precedents which are too remote to be of much relevance today – the last royal calling of a dissolution was by William IV in 1834, and the last refusal of a commission to form a government was by Lord Hartington in 1880. Our precedents are shaped by a two-party norm. The problem of whether a minority government can claim a dissolution when the Parliament contains an alternative grouping commanding a clear majority has never been put to the test. New rules are needed, preferably after public discussion, well in advance of any crisis.

But are the rules about dissolution really critical? It can be argued that in practice no one is likely to call an election gratuitously. Elections are not, in themselves, popular and the public may be unlikely to reward a politician or a party that inflicts one on them unnecessarily, as is demonstrated by the worldwide reluctance to call a second election quickly.[12] The main safeguard against a Prime Minister defeated on the first Queen's Speech of a Parliament calling another election is probably his own instinct for survival.

Could or should the sovereign contemplate refusing such a request? By one theory, of course, the Queen can refuse a dissolution just as she can veto an Act of Parliament. But royal powers unused for a very long period are widely thought to have withered away. Despite what Sir Alan Lascelles wrote in 1950, it does seem that a majority of constitutional lawyers and political observers would hold it to be ill-advised, and indeed improper, for the Queen to refuse a dissolution to a duly appointed Prime Minister, even if he had never had the endorsement of the House of Commons.[13]

Could she make it a condition at the time of appointment that there should be no question of dissolution if the Prime

Minister failed to muster a parliamentary majority? The behaviour of George V in 1910 (when he made his promise to create the peers that might be needed to pass the Parliament Act dependent on first having an election with a favourable verdict) is the nearest example in this century of the sovereign laying down conditions about accepting Prime Ministerial advice on the use of the royal prerogative. But the imposition on a potential Prime Minister of a condition about not demanding a dissolution would be necessary only if there was reason to suppose that he might, in fact, make such a request; for the sovereign to lay down terms at such a moment would undoubtedly involve the sovereign in political controversy. The matter might be better left to the voters; an appeal to the electorate is always proper although, as Markesinis points out, 'a series of dissolutions, particularly if they were based on the same reason, might represent a triumph over, and not a triumph of, the electorate.'[14]

The problem raised by the Lascelles letter remains. It would surely be wrong for a minority party in a new Parliament to inflict another election on the people if the Parliament did contain a viable majority. On the other hand, if one newly designated Prime Minister, defeated at the first vote in the House of Commons, asks for and is refused a dissolution, can there be any certainty that the next nominee will be able to put together a Commons majority? Would he then also be refused a dissolution because a third attempt at government-forming might be successful? There might, however, come a moment when it was plain that the only resolution to the crisis lay in a new election. Who would fight the election as Prime Minister, with all the advantages that go with possession of the office? The sovereign who refused a dissolution to A and then to B, may be called partisan for, in the end, giving it to C; as Markesinis puts it, 'the Crown would be placed "in the intolerable and dangerous position?" of granting to one Prime Minister what it had recently refused to another.'[15]

One way out of this dilemma seems attractive. The Palace could intimate (during a time of political peace, when it could not be seen who might be advantaged or hurt by the decision) that a dissolution would be granted only when it was plain that there was no possibility of a majority government emerging from the current House. Such an intimation could, of course, come in response to a resolution from Parliament but, equally, it might be volunteered. The sovereign, without abandoning any formal prerogative, would be making plain the neutral way in which the umpire's role would be exercised. Just as the Speaker exercises his casting vote on principles laid down in Erskine May's *Parliamentary Practice* and escapes all suspicion of partiality, so the Palace, by setting out its mechanical decision rules in advance, can avoid embarrassing imputations.

One device, suggested in 1974, has its possibilities. A no confidence motion could contain within its wording a humble suggestion that, if it was carried, the Prime Minister should not be granted a dissolution. Formally the House of Commons has no authority over the sovereign and the use of the royal prerogative cannot be the subject of debate. But nothing in Standing Orders would prevent the House from expressing its desires, even if the passage of the motion could have no binding force on the sovereign.

This would not go so far as the rule in countries where the legislature can be dissolved before the statutory end of its four-year term only if there is a clear majority vote by its own members. If this were accepted practice in Britain, the sovereign would be freed from the possibility of having to exercise a potentially embarrassing discretion.

To refer all decisions over dissolution to the House of Commons does not guarantee a solution to all crises. It is hypothetically possible to conceive of a House of Commons that refused to vote for its own dissolution, even though it was unable to produce a viable government from its current membership. No set of rules can save a democracy from a totally obstinate refusal to compromise by its politicians. However, the dilemma envisaged here has not, in fact, been a problem in any of the Commonwealth or European countries with a comparable parliamentary system. Crises do get solved, usually fairly quickly, either by the emergence of a coalition or a minority government with a reasonable expectation of life, or by a dissolution. And politicians are always inhibited in criticizing a dissolution; what, after all, is a dissolution but the referring of a political problem to the decision of the politicians' ultimate 'sovereign' – the people?

It is worth restating the central argument of this chapter. It accepts that when a government-forming crisis arises, the most obvious problem for the Palace is whom to consult and whom then to call upon to form a government. But it focuses upon the subsidiary dilemmas: upon the remit to be given to the *formateur* and, in particular, upon his right to ask for a dissolution. These problems could be simply solved without legislation, and without infringement of the royal prerogative. All that would be required would be for the Palace to let it be known, firstly, that in future anyone asked to try to form a government would receive the seals of office only after there had been an affirmative motion from the House of Commons endorsing the nomination, or, secondly, that a request for dissolution would be granted only in response to a vote by the House of Commons. The first of these practices would, by itself, remove the possibility of a Prime Ministerial nominee who had never commanded a Commons majority, snatching an unreasonable advantage by a snap dissolution. The second would be more far-reaching in that it would influence much more than the first moments of a government's life. If dissolution always required the consent of the Commons, then a cabinet crisis in mid-Parliament would be more likely to be solved without recourse to the electorate. For good or ill, a government defeated in a Commons vote could have a dissolution only if there were no alternative government available. In normal circumstances, of course, the institution of these practices would make no significant difference to the authority of a Prime Minister in full control of a majority party.[16] But in marginal situations, such customs would free the sovereign from the burden of making what some might see as a partisan decision. The constitution is, by its nature, in a state of constant development. This is one area where its evolution might, with benefit to all, be consciously accelerated.

CHAPTER EIGHT

Wider Considerations

―――――•◦•―――――

IF THE GENERAL ELECTION OF 1983-4, or that of 1987-8, produces
no clear parliamentary majority, the situation may well be
seen as a one-off event, a problem to be solved in an *ad hoc*
fashion just as it was in 1923, 1929, 1974 and 1977. It will
present some of the problems which have been discussed in
the previous chapters but, if everybody regards what is
happening as a transient aberration, it will not change the
nature of British politics. If it is accepted that the following
election is likely to reinstate majority government with all its
conventions, parties and institutions will tread water until
the *status quo* is restored.

If, however, it becomes apparent that minority or
coalition government is becoming the norm rather than the
exception in British politics, then many further problems
will come to the fore. If two-party dominance ends, either
through a break-up of existing voting patterns, or through
the adoption of proportional representation, many routine
assumptions about the working of the British government
will have to be challenged.

This chapter explores some of them. Few people realize
how deeply engrained and how permeating are the notions
that go with the adversary politics of two parties, alternating
in power. There are virtually no sections in any standard
textbook on British government that would not have to be
rewritten in a world of permanently hung parliaments.

It should be stressed that, in what follows, the story will
be different if hung parliaments arise from intra-party splits

135

and realignments (which may, after all, be as passing a phase as they were in the 1850s or the 1920s), or if hung parliaments result from the adoption of proportional representation with all its implications for permanent minority or coalition governments. And the impact of proportional representation, especially for the working of parties, will depend greatly upon the variant of proportional representation which is adopted.[1]

When the framework of institutions changes, it often takes those involved a long time to recognize what has happened. As Bagehot wrote in 1868:

> A new Constitution does not produce its full effect as long as all its subjects were reared under an old Constitution, as long as its statesmen were trained by that old Constitution. It is not really tested till it comes to be worked by statesmen and among a people, neither of whom were guided by the old experience.[2]

The learning curve may be rather faster in the 1980s, but it will still take years for new habits of conduct to develop and new constitutional conventions to be generally accepted.

Collective responsibility

The doctrine of collective responsibility could not be fully sustained if two or more autonomous parties were involved in every government. Inevitably there would be an increased amount of leaking about stances within the cabinet. The rank and file of each coalition party would suspect that their leaders were selling out to, or being hoodwinked by, their partners; cabinet members would be under enormous pressure to show that they had done their best and had come out well from the necessary compromises of cabinet. Moreover, when the government was in trouble, the temptation to make a scapegoat of the other partner or partners, would be enormous. The Prime Minister would be even more powerless than at present to stop cabinet leaks, since ministers from another party would be difficult to transfer or to sack.

The forms of collective responsibility can, of course, be formally maintained with a coalition government. All the democracies of Scandinavia and the Low Countries claim to preserve collective responsibility fairly strictly. But, especially as an election approaches, it would be too much to expect that all cabinet members would be willing to accept full and equal responsibility for every action of the government, especially ones that involved major deviations from their own party's policy.

Sometimes a licence to differ publicly would have to be given, as it was in 1931-2 or in 1975. Sometimes the survival of a coalition would be achieved by referring a contentious issue to a free vote or to a referendum. And, usually, in the absence of such devices, an instinct for self-preservation would moderate any flaunting of cabinet splits: the party leaders, if they wanted the coalition to continue, would try to curtail internal disputes. In a war of leaks it is easy for escalation to set in; the opposition and the political correspondents naturally delight in ferreting out evidence of disunity. The glue of self-interest will hold together a coalition cabinet, just as it enables a one-party cabinet to maintain a moderate degree of discretion. But with a coalition the glue will be much weaker.

Individual responsibilty

Coalition government would not, in itself, impair the central tenets of the doctrine of the individual responsibility of ministers: that for every action of a servant of the Crown a minister must answer in Parliament; that civil servants are anonymous – ministers get the credit when they do things right and take the blame when they do things wrong; that civil servants are non-political and, irrespective of any private views, do their best for any political master.

However, in a coalition, both within and between departments, ministers of different parties will note the views of their advisers and when rifts appear between coalition partners, civil servants may find it difficult to maintain the appearance of neutrality. When, furthermore, there is a partial realignment of coalition partners in mid Parliament, the theory that a minister cannot see his predecessor's papers or identify the advice that his present advisers were once giving, may be difficult to implement.

Moreover, in a large department with different ministers being allocated subsidiary empires, the Secretary of State may be reluctant to accept full public responsibility for everything that goes on, since his junior colleagues may come from a different party and be personally or ideologically at odds with him. In a coalition there would certainly be less mutual trust than in a one-party administration. Every Secretary of State would be worried about what his junior ministers from other parties were up to. Interdepartmental negotiations at the ministerial level might well be channelled along party lines. When confronted with the spectre of coalition government with ministerial masters from different parties, one senior civil servant remarked, 'It would mean a lot more work for us – and probably, when you come to think of it, a lot more power for us.' There would probably be a strongly renewed thrust for more outsiders to be brought in as special advisers. At the moment only ministers at the head of departments are allowed such assistance. But in a coalition government, some at least of the middle-rank ministers would stake out their own claim. How, in a large department, could a Secretary of State of Party A, with his special adviser, be balanced by a number two from Party B, who lacked such support? It is clear that departmental politics will become much more active.

The power of the chamber

Collective responsiblity would also be eroded by the inevitable increase in the power of Parliament. Just as the Labour Government in 1974-9 accepted defeat on a number of issues that, in former days, might have been regarded as issues of confidence, so any future coalition or minority government would be tempted, or forced, to solve difficult issues by leaving the decision to Parliament. And opposition parties might not find it difficult to locate co-operative dissidents within one or other of the coalition parties.

The strength of whipping would depend upon the electoral system and the method of party organization. List Systems of PR conduce to party discipline, while the Single Transferable Vote fosters individualism among MPs. But there is little doubt that, in a minority situation, governments would have to yield to the will of the House much more than they do now.

Select Committees

The power of Commons' committees, though still limited, seems to have grown since the reforms of 1980. In a coalition situation, particularly if there were frequent reshuffles, the influence of committees would be bound to grow. An increasingly independent House would be more ready to support an alternative policy, emanating from the relevant committee, against a departmental view. Governments would not be able to slap down committee reports so readily or even, indeed, to resist demands for more ample staffing of committees in a way that would increase the scale and the persuasiveness of their reports. There might well be an increase in the proportion of MPs who saw their political fulfilment coming from committee chairmanship rather than from the achievement of ministerial office.

It is also worth noting that committees would not have

one-party majorities. They already have a tendency to be remarkably non-partisan but, in a coalition world, there would be even less chance of their being nobbled by the government whips.

The role of the opposition

Britain is unique among European democracies in having a paid office of Leader of the Opposition. Among other things, he allocates opposition time in Parliament not only for his own, the largest opposition party, but for the minor parties as well. He is at the head of a shadow cabinet, a government in exile that mirrors the real cabinet, with shadow portfolios and even a doctrine of collective responsibility.

If the parties were more equal in numbers, the very post of Leader of the Opposition might have to be rethought. Consider two election outcomes:

TABLE 18
Two hypothetical election outcomes

Majority government		Minority government	
Party A	330 seats	Party A	280 seats
Party B	146 seats	Party B	176 seats
Party C	145 seats	Party C	175 seats
Others	29 seats	Others	29 seats

In neither situation would it be obvious that Party B constituted the alternative government, and the most likely next holder of power. In neither situation would it be acceptable for the fractionally larger of the opposition groupings to have the authority that Erskine May currently assigns to the Leader of the Opposition in regard to the disposal of House of Commons time and facilities.

There is also a problem for the Speaker. The ministers of the Crown Act of 1937 requires him to designate as Leader of the Opposition the leader of the party, 'having the greatest numerical strength in the House'. If, in either of these examples, two minor-party MPs defected to Party C or if there were a couple of by-election vacancies, would the office and its perquisites be switched? And what would be the position of a declared party alliance? If the Liberals and Social Democrats fought an election together and jointly emerged with more seats than, say, Labour, would their agreed leader get the post, or would it go to Labour as the largest single grouping? Would a defeated coalition government form a coalition shadow cabinet when it moved to the opposition benches?

There is a more fundamental question. We normally think of the Opposition as the group of MPs who believe that the government should be thrown out and that they should take their places. And, sooner or later, every opposition front bench has moved across to the Treasury side. But in hung parliaments that will not necessarily be the pattern of governmental change. As in most continental countries, a more co-operative style of politics may develop, in which a single Leader of the Opposition, one pre-eminent licenced adversary, may seem inappropriate. In a world of hung parliaments, parties outside government will still strive for office and government policies will be opposed. But parliamentary opposition will, to some extent at least, move from the stylized and always unsuccessful attempts to secure the total rejection of government measures, with which we are familiar and which take up so much of the time of the House of Commons. There will, inevitably, be more serious efforts at persuasion and amendment. In a situation where parties are always going to need allies, the ritual excesses of parliamentary rhetoric may sound inappropriate. In all sorts of ways, MPs will have to learn a new approach if they are to be effective in a world without majorities.

Pressure groups

In Washington lobbyists seek the votes of congressmen. But in Westminster the whips have safeguarded MPs from such pressures. Governments treat all major measures as issues of confidence. Except on the occasional private member's bill, the outcome of a parliamentary division can never be decided by persuasions to individual members. But, if it becomes accepted that governments can accept defeat, voting will become less predictable. It will become much more worth while for interest groups of every sort to bring to bear on MPs intellectual arguments or other pressures. Debate in the chamber, solicitation in the lobbies, and constituency mail will each be influential. The role of the lobbyist will necessarily grow.

Party policy

With or without proportional representation, if coalition government becomes the norm, it will change party approaches to policy-making. At the moment parties put forward policies which they believe they can put into effect and, if they win a clear majority, they know that they will largely be judged by their success in doing so. If they have no hope of gaining full power, will they become more responsible in their promises, or less? They may be tempted to promise more because, if they take a share of office but leave pledges unfulfilled, they can blame their coalition partners. They may prudently promise less because they want to be seen as realistic, and because their manifesto becomes a negotiating brief for their government-forming talks with potential partners. It has been argued that coalitions have both a centripetal and a centrifugal effect;

centripetal in that they force parties into a narrower, more pragmatic range of co-operative endeavour; centrifugal in that they encourage irresponsible, unredeemable pledges. It has also been argued that coalitions make parties more ideological. Since elections cease to be a choice between alternative governments, each with their complete manifesto, they become more an affair of philosophy, a recording of political tendency, an assertion of the voter's personal position on the political spectrum. It is impossible to say whether British parties would move in the pragmatic or the ideological direction. Habits change very slowly. In many ways the discourse of politics would continue as before. But those engaged in preparing party policies and those presenting them would certainly have to think afresh about the nature of their task.

Party structures

If coalition government were associated with proportional representation, the organization of parties would have to change. Every form of proportional representation require larger constituencies. Even with the Additional Member System, as used in West Germany, each constituency would be twice as big, while the Single Transferable Vote, as used in Ireland, or the Regional List as proposed for the European Parliament, would demand far larger basic units for the selection of candidates and the organization of campaigns. Any list or multi-member constituency system involves the choice of teams as distinct from individual candidates. The ladders of advancement would be different and the personnel of politics would change. Parties would pursue balanced tickets and the opportunities for women and for members of racial and religious minorities to get into Parliament would be much enhanced. Well-known names would be at a great advantage, because in large constituencies there are obvious attractions in having a nationally known name on a party list, perhaps one originally made familiar in the world of sport or entertainment. The changed composition of Parliament, with a broader range of representation, might be for good or for ill. It would not be negligible.

Institutional change

If there were two or three successive parliaments with no clear majorities, it is almost inevitable that there would be a change in the electoral system which will guarantee the continuance of hung parliaments. And in such a situation some of the often-voiced demands for a change in institutions will gain new force. The advocates of a Bill of Rights, a written constitution and a reformed second chamber, not to mention devolution and new arrangements for local government, would get a more influential platform. The need to get coalition support for any change might prove a conservative, obstructive influence. Yet in the trade-offs of party co-operation, the pet nostrums of one party might often win out and, as part of a government-forming deal, get carried through with majority support.

It has been observed that 'coalition government might purge or it might constipate'. That is a matter of guesswork. What is certain is that it would have a far-reaching effect on our political culture and our national cohesion. This has been a pragmatic book written to stimulate discussion about problems that may suddenly afflict British politics. It has been composed with a full awareness that these problems will, in the end, be solved 'by guess and by God' when they actually arise: politicians will improvise and set their own precedents as they attempt to solve each immediate difficulty in their own or their party's interests. But it has also been composed in the belief that prior discussion of the problems may close off some blind alleys and define some paths that may lead to constructive solutions.

Overseas experience has much to offer. Institutions can

never be exported whole from one country to another – but devices evolved in one national laboratory can often be adapted to quite different conditions.

The 1980s may pass without providing an example of hung parliaments – although, as Chapter 2 showed, that is much less likely than most people realize. The problems that hung parliaments would cause may resolve themselves much more simply than has been envisaged here – or in quite different ways. But they are problems that are likely to reverberate through the world of practical politics, as well as of political science, in the years to come, perhaps immediately but certainly in the next decade or two. They are problems that will be solved better, and with less recrimination, if they are thought about now.

NOTES

Chapter 2

1 In this and later tables Northern Ireland has been excluded because its   22
elections have been fought on a basis so completely different from that in
Britain. This table is drawn from the important article by John Curtice
and Michael Steed which provides the basis for many of the points in this
chapter. See 'Electoral Choice and the Production of Government: The
Changing Operation of the Electoral System in the United Kingdom since
1955', *British Journal of Political Science, 12*, 249-298, Summer 1982.

2 The two-party vote is a concept developed by Michael Steed. Each   25
party's support is recorded as a percentage not of the total vote cast but
of the sum of Conservative and Labour votes.

3 These results may not be as capricious as they seem. They may reflect   33
a conscious change in the way the Irish allocated their second and later
preference votes between 1969 and 1973.

Chapter 3

1 D. Marquand in D. Butler (ed.) *Coalitions in British Politics*, London   46
1978, p.58.

2 A.J.P.Taylor ibid. p.74.   49

3 D. Steel, *A House Divided*, London 1980, pp.153-7. See also A. Michie   54
and S. Hoggart, *The Pact*, London 1978.

Chapter 4

1 *Ministrable* and *non-ministrable* are convenient French terms to describe   63
politicians who are, or who are not, regarded as suitable for ministerial
office.

2 France and Portugal would provide exceptions to this statement if we   63
were considering them here.

3 William Riker sets out this principle formally: 71
In N-person, zero-sum games, where side payments are permitted,

where players are rational and where they have perfect information, only minimum winning coalitions occur.
W. Riker, *The Theory of Political Coalitions*, New Haven and London, 1962.

4 Eric C. Browne and John Dreijmanis (eds.), *Government Coalitions in*   71
Western Democracies London 1982, p.336.

Chapter 5

1 W.I. Jennings, *Cabinet Government* 3rd ed., London 1959, p.57.   79

2 It may be worth noting that similar charges are made against the   81
judiciary, but that does not lead to any widespread challenge to the
umpire role of the courts.

3 L. S. Amery claims that in May 1923 he and Bridgeman, another junior   82
member of the cabinet, changed the course of history. They button-holed
Lord Stamfordham, George V's Private Secretary, in St James's Park just
when Lord Curzon was going to be sent for and argued that Baldwin
would be a better Prime Minister. Further consultations followed and in
the end Baldwin was summoned. See L. S. Amery, *Diaries*, London 1980,
Vol.1, p.327. But Lord Stamfordham's note on the subject throws doubt
on the importance of Amery's intervention. See R. Blake, *The Unknown
Prime Minister* London 1955, p.527.

In January 1924 Lord Stamfordham wrote to Professor A.F. Pollard,
whom he did not know, asking him for the full text of a lecture on the power
of dissolution, which had been briefly reported in *The Times*.

4 In Britain the Palace might also find it prudent to indicate that personal   83
and administrative convenience would affect the sequence of interview so
that no deep significance should be read into the fact that A saw the Queen
before B or that C seemed to be at the back of the queue.

5 Tony Benn 'Power, Parliament and the People' *New Socialist* Sept-Oct   84
1982, p.14.

6 *Guardian*, 24 August 1982.   87

7 It was probably not asked in the intra-party transitions of 1955, 1957,   91
and 1976. Only in 1963 did the Queen definitely receive advice: Mr
Macmillan from his hospital bed told her, in the light of the soundings
by the whips and the party officials, to send for Lord Home. Now that
party leaders are elected, it is unlikely that there would be much deviation
from the pattern of 1976, when Mr Wilson stayed in office till the party
had chosen his successor. Problems might arise if a Prime Minister died
in office, particularly with Labour where the new processes of mass
election would have to take several weeks.

8 W.I. Jennings *Cabinet Government*, 3rd ed., London 1959, p.42.   91

9 Ibid. p.40.   91

10 In the last 25 years, the only examples of 2 elections within 12 months   95
are provided by: Ireland 1981-2 (8 months) and 1982 (9 months); Canada
1979-80 (7 months); Japan 1979-80 (8 months); United Kingdom 1974
(7 months); Greece 1963-4 (3 months). Greece offers the only example of
two elections within six months.

11 Another way of putting the question is to ask whether, if the 11 Ulster   102
Unionists had been willing to accept the Conservative Whip, would Mr
Heath who 'lost' by 297 to 301 to Harold Wilson, have 'won' by 308 to
301?

12 Nigerian Federal Supreme Court, 187/1962   106

13 [1963] A.C. 614 at p.631-2 : quoted by Zelman Cowan in his   108
introduction to the second edition of H.V. Evatt *The King and his Dominion
Governors*, London 1967.

Chapter 6

1 It might, however, be observed that if Mrs Thatcher's government were   116
to be regarded as a coalition, by 1982 the dries had got the economic
departments while the wets were exiled to Northern Ireland and to
Agriculture. If Harold Wilson's Labour administrations were coalitions,
the Gaitskellites pre-empted the Treasury area.

Chapter 7

1 H.V. Evatt, *The King and his Dominion Governors* 2nd ed. London 1967;   123
E.A. Forsey, *The Royal Power of Dissolution of Parliament in the British
Commonwealth* Oxford 1943; B.S. Markesinis, *The Theory and Practice of
Dissolution of Parliament*, Cambridge 1972.

2 *The Law of the Constitution*, 10th ed., London 1967, p.424, p.428-9.   123

3 *Law and Custom of the Constitution*, Oxford, 4th ed. 1911, p.432-3.   123

4 *Letters of Queen Victoria*, 1st series III, London 1907, p.363.   124

5 Letter in *The Times*, 13 May 1969.   124

6 Quoted by R. Blake *The Unknown Prime Minister*, London 1955, p.152.   124

7 H. Nicolson, *King George V*, London 1952, p.379.   124

8 J.A. Spender, *Life of Lord Oxford and Asquith*, London 1932, Vol.II,   125
pp.30-31.

9 *The Times*, 19 Dec 1923.   126

10 *The Times*, 24 Apr 1950.   127

11 See John Kerr, *Matters for Judgment*, Melbourne 1978 and London   129

1979; and Gough Whitlam, *The Truth of the Matter*, Ringwood, Vic. 1979, for the views of the main protagonists. See G. Sawer *Federation under Strain*, Ringwood, Vic.1979, for the most dispassionate of the many assessments of the crisis.

12 See footnote 10, Chapter 5. However, the United Kingdom does have   130 one odd liability to two elections in very quick succession. The Meeting of Parliament Act of 1797 is still on the Statute Book. It provides that if the sovereign dies at any point between the dissolution of Parliament and the day appointed for the meeting of its successor the election becomes void and the old Parliament has to reassemble. That Act has never been repealed. The contingency envisaged is a remote one, although it did come within four months of occurring in 1951-2. But it opens the startling possibility of a completed election being voided by the death of the sovereign in the two weeks between polling day and the assembling of Parliament. Indeed a Prime Minister who had called an election and lost but who had not yet resigned, might find himself tempted to soldier on. Perhaps the Law Commission should include the 1797 Act, or parts of it, in their next list of obsolete laws overdue for repeal.

13 It is, however, worth noting that the Deputy Leader of the Labour   130 Party, Edward Short, wrote to Norman Atkinson on 9 May 1974:
> Constitutional Lawyers of the highest authority are of the clear opinion that the Sovereign is not in all circumstances bound to grant a Prime Minister's request for a dissolution.

quoted in *The Times* 11 May 1974.

14 B.S. Markesinis, *The Theory and Practice of the Dissolution of Parliament*,   131 Cambridge 1972, p.120.

15 Ibid. p.89.   132

16 It might however be a nuisance to reassemble Parliament in   134 September just to clear the way for an October dissolution. But this, *de facto*, was done in 1951.

Chapter 8

1 For a discussion of the technicalities and consequences of various forms   136 of proportional representation see S.E. Finer, *Adversary Politics and Electoral Reform*, London 1975; Enid Lakeman, *Power to Elect*, London 1982; V. Bogdanor and D. Butler, *Democracy and Elections*, Cambridge 1983.

2 Walter Bagehot, Introduction to the Second Edition of *The English*   136 *Constitution*, London 1867.

BIBLIOGRAPHY

Anson, W.A., *Law and Custom of the Constitution*, 4th ed., London 1911.

Axelrod, R. *Conflict of Interest*, Chicago, 1970.

Bogdanor, V. and Butler, D. *Democracy and Elections*, Cambridge 1983.

Browne, E.C. and Dreijmanis, J. (eds.) *Government Coalitions in Western Democracies*, London 1982.

Butler, D. (ed.) *Coalitions in British Politics*, London 1978.

Dicey, A.V. *The Law of the Constitution*, 10th ed., London 1967.

Dodd, L.C. *Coalitions in Parliamentary Government*, Princeton N.J. 1976.

Evatt, H.V. *The King and his Dominion Governors*, 2nd ed., London 1967.

Finer, S.E. (ed.) *Adversary Politics and Electoral Reform*, London 1975.

Forsey, E. *The Royal Power of Dissolution in the British Commonwealth*, Oxford 1943.

Groenings, S., Kelley, E.W., and Leiserson, M. *The Study of Coalition Behavior*, New York 1970.

Jennings, W.I. *Cabinet Government*, 3rd ed., London 1959.

Mackintosh, J. *The British Cabinet*, 3rd ed. London 1977.

Markesinis, B.S. *The Theory and Practice of the Dissolution of Parliament*, Cambridge 1972.

Maude, A. and Szemerey, J. *Why Electoral Change?* London 1982.

Michie, A. and Hoggart S.   *The Pact*, London 1978.

Riker, W.H.   *The Theory of Political Coalitions*, New Haven and London 1962.

Schelling, T.   *The Strategy of Conflict*, Cambridge, Mass. 1958.

Steel, D.   *A House Divided*, London 1980.

INDEX